THE BEATIN' PATH
a lyrical guide to lucid evolution

JOHN B LANE

Global Arts Ltd
3531 South Logan St D-193
Englewood, Colorado 80113
USA

Design by Anile Prakash

The Beatin' Path is typeset in Fern, designed by David Jonathan Ross. Used with permission from The Font Bureau, Inc.

First edition January 2017

Library of Congress Control Number: 2016920210

ISBN: 978-0-9984356-3-3
ISBN: 978-0-9984356-1-9 (ebook)

www.thebeatinpath.com

Along the way...

Are we here yet?

Bullshit doesn't age well.

Make things better!

The Beatin' Path

Mantra for a Panther in a Room Full of Metronomes

Do not fear
the path you walk,
for fear will not protect you;
the path won't misdirect...
you already *have* your place in space/time.

Now
breath in...
now exhale...
then is now
and then again,
breathing in,
then letting go,
only to begin
again...

A Way We Go

And so, we are here, my friend.
We are alive, are we not?
What shall we do?

Shall we *wither* together?
Exist until we die?
Expect little of ourselves?
Accept what falls into our hands, our hearts, our minds?
Shall we pass our days without noticing or engaging with
the world that waits around us?

Or shall we *seek*?
Shall we bloom?
Shall we rise up and open our eyes?
Embrace the beauty and the challenge?
Shall we live this life *con gusto*?
Shall we pursue our full potential?
Expand our expectations?
Shall we grow and seize the wonder that is life?

The open mind says, 'Hai!'
The open mind yearns for more.
The open mind understands
that the kingdom of heaven is at hand.
Here. Now. Always.
For the discovery.
For the learning.
For the *earning*.
In this moment.
In the next moment.
In the moment after that.
It is within us so to do.
Upon the beatin' path, *proceed...*

ARE WE HERE YET?

A Most Revolutionary Question

A GREAT SAGE NAMED SATCHEL PAIGE
once asked a question for the ages:

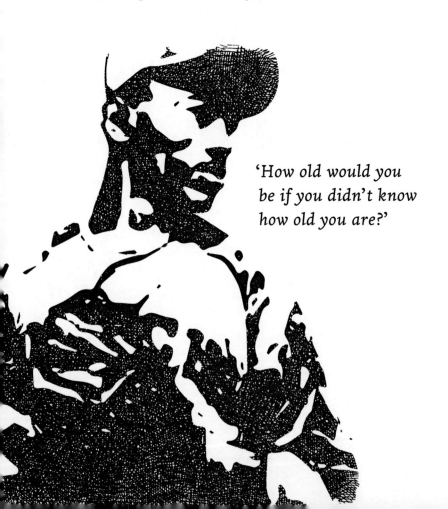

'How old would you
be if you didn't know
how old you are?'

We might ponder the meaning of that question
for years! 'I feel like I'm 40,' the 54-year-
old man might say. 'I wish I was 25,' his wife
might reply. Those are reasonable answers
to what seems such a simple question.

But within that question, old Satchel was throwing
his most unhittable change-up ever. He'd watched
the prime years of his youth melt away, pitching
in the Negro Leagues. Because although he'd
been born with one of the liveliest arms the game
of baseball has ever seen, the pigment of his
skin was not up to the standards of the day.

By the time a more enlightened consciousness
overtook the society in which he lived, by the time
he had a chance to perform on the more widely-
known stage of the major leagues, his physical
skills had begun to fade. He was celebrated for how
great he *might* have been, not for the greatness he
was able to *demonstrate* to the baseball masses.

Satchel Paige's insights and wisdom did *not*
fade, however, for time is on the side of those
who learn from their experiences. So the offhand
craftiness of his question must have come to Mr
Paige with the same instincts he would have used
in sizing up a hitter who was two strikes in the
hole – then winding up and throwing the least
hittable pitch, in the least-expected location.

'How old would you be if you didn't know how old
you are?' It might be the most revolutionary question

ever asked, because it challenges the questionee
to step outside of all the artificial assumptions
imposed, in the most constant, imperceptible,
and overwhelming ways, on every individual
who lives long enough to learn how to count.

Assumptions attach themselves from all directions
– from family, from friends, from authorities, from
enemies, from lovers...and most fatally, from
within. These assumptions dictate and constrain our
thoughts and behaviors, our dreams and expectations.
Few are able, or willing, to venture beyond the
assumptions of the soil in which they are planted.
Few are even *aware* of the assumptions that limit
and control them, in the same way that fish are
unaware of the medium we recognize as 'water'.

It cannot be argued that certain assumptions
are essential in order for two or more people to
live together with a reasonable degree of civility.
We must not physically harm one another, for
example. We must not steal from others.

But we have been busy these last few thousand
years! Busy inventing unnecessary layers of
restraint, which limit our minds and our souls.
Generation after generation, these layers, which
we accept without consideration, provide a
superficial comfort. They mold us and allow us to
resemble those around us, and thereby to earn the
acceptance of those whose acceptance we value.

In return, we surrender our most precious

gifts as humans. We lock our minds and our souls inside society-shaped cages, and spend the rest of our lives ignoring the bars. So when someone asks us how old we'd be if we didn't know how old we are, it's like asking what we'll do with our lives once we get out of prison.

'What prison?'

Wings, that I Might Walk

I MET A BIRD WHO WOULDN'T FLY. I couldn't understand the reason why.

I asked him if his wings were broken. And though he seemed to be well-spoken, his words still make no sense to me.

'I walk the Earth to atone for the indiscretion of the first two birds,' he said. 'Their crime is mine, in the sense that I inherited their guilt – which I accept, of course. How could I in good faith deny responsibility for the mistake of my original ancestors? Am I not my great, great, great ^{1,000,000} grandparents' keeper?'

'Can you tell me of their fateful deed?' I asked the bird as he rubbed his tired feet.

'I can paraphrase,' he said, 'though you'll find the official version by God Himself if you take the time to read the Wholly Babble. You see, He created my great, great, great ^{1,000,000} grandmother and grandfather to tend his tranquil garden. He was tired from the toil, and planned to rest the rest of His eternity along the sunny *Cote d'Azur*.

'And why not? Having just created everything, had He
not earned the pleasure that His leisure now would
bring? He planned to paint and swim and maybe open a
boutique winery in the hills above the sea. But none of
this was meant to be. And now it all comes down to me.

'You see, He entrusted His peaceful paradise in the
wings of my great, great, great ^{1,000,000} grandparents,
with but one simple stipulation: they were not,
under any circumstance, to eat of the sunflower
of the knowledge of Will and Orville. For if
they did, on that day they would surely die.

'I am left to wonder why, of all the things they could have done, they did not do them all, but *not* the one.'

He raised a wing to brush a sudden tear that almost overflowed his eye. 'Instead, they happened upon a worm (*Curse the day!*) who said, "I have travelled from one end of this garden to another, and I have never found a better taste than the seed of yon sunflower. It is delicious, it is nutritious, and in your case, it is indeed, *auspicious*."

'"*But...*" said my great, great, great ^{1,000,000} grandmother.

'"I know what you're going to say," the worm interrupted. "You were told that should you partake of the sunflower of the knowledge of Will and Orville, that on that day you would surely die. May I assure my feathered friends, that statement is a lie."

'At this same time, I picture God unfurling a towel upon the sand, thinking, now, at last and finally, *retirement* was at hand.

'Instead, to our eternal shame, my great, great,
great ^{1,000,000} grandparents chose the weaker path,
to taste the forbidden seed. And in that moment,
they understood the potential in their wings.
They uplifted their befeathered arms and left the
safety of the Earth behind. The sky itself became
their home, where only God had ever roamed.

'Of all the creatures great and small, only two had wings,
and what wonders did those wings reveal! Existence
had a third dimension, and all the complications
down below gave way to the understanding that all
were simply parts of a delicate and glorious whole.

'They soared above the mountains and the rivers
and the fertile fields of grass. And when the day had
come to pass, they landed safely in a banyan tree. Oh,
what a wondrous place this world could ever be!

'God stood beside the tree, filled with emotion, as
anyone would be. Angry, betrayed, embarrassed
(at the fact they did not die), and resentful at the
permanent interruption of His permanent vacation.

'"You have disobeyed Me!" He said,
redundantly. "As your punishment, I forbid
you from flying, for all eternity."

'My great, great, great ^{1,000,000} grandparents felt
ashamed. They knew they'd violated the confines of
dimensions one and two. And so they climbed down

from the tree and they agreed to never fly again.

'It isn't easy,' said the bird, lifting a weak and
weary wing to shade the sunshine from his eyes.
'Sometimes I think these scrawny feet weren't
exactly made for *walkin'*. But what better way
to repay the debt? It's the least that I can do.'

He cast a wistful glance to a cloud on the horizon, then
off on foot he set. 'Wish me luck,' he said. 'I've got
birds to see in Bermondsey, next Saturday at three.'

'You could be there in half a day if you fly!'

He cocked his head and looked at me as if I'd
crossed my eyes. 'Why would the Good Lord
give me feet, if He had wanted me to fly?'

To this, alas, I could muster no reply.

Miasma

 DEAS CAN BE PRISONS. Some ideas might seem crazy from the outside, but make good sense to the people who believe them.

Do men look wise and powerful in powdered wigs...or do they simply look absurd? It depends on whom you ask, and when.

A *style* is an idea with a short shelf life.

DOES THIS WIG MAKE ME LOOK ABSURD?

People used to think the world was flat, and if you wandered off too far...that you wouldn't be wandering *back*. Oh, it seems like a reasonable idea! If the world was anything *but* flat, would all of us *not* fall off?

It was the best way to explain the way things were...until we acquired a better understanding of gravity and geography. In other words, it was a reasonable idea, until better reasons came along. That's the way that knowledge works.

Now, the 'Flat Earth Society' is a genteel name for those who cling to *extinct* ideas.

Conventional wisdom once was convinced that humans were *physically incapable* of running a mile in less than four minutes. And then on the 6th of May in 1954, Roger Bannister ran a mile in 3:59.4.

Not long after that, it was common for elite runners to break four minutes, almost as though the *idea itself* had been the barrier, not the physical limitations of the human body.

Ideas – the things we tell ourselves – *matter*. If you find yourself lost in the woods, you'll have a better chance of surviving if you tell yourself you *will* survive. Positive self-talk is an idea that might save your life...

up to a point. Once you pass that point, all the positive thinking in the world won't substitute for a drink of water.

The difference between whether

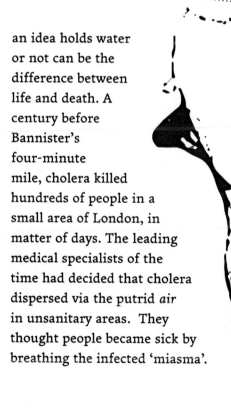

3:59.4

an idea holds water or not can be the difference between life and death. A century before Bannister's four-minute mile, cholera killed hundreds of people in a small area of London, in matter of days. The leading medical specialists of the time had decided that cholera dispersed via the putrid *air* in unsanitary areas. They thought people became sick by breathing the infected 'miasma'.

Though it was an idea that wasn't formed by facts, it *could have been* correct. But it *wasn't*. So while the 'experts' rested, falsely confident, the afflicted...? They rested, truly *permanent*.

A physician named John Snow decided to ignore the persistent ignorance of the miasma theory and the influential people who accepted it. Instead, Dr Snow became a *detective*. He gathered evidence, and followed its trail to the truth.

His methods, and the map in which he documented cholera cases near Broad Street

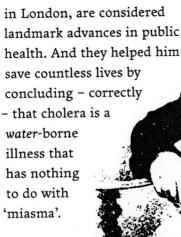

in London, are considered landmark advances in public health. And they helped him save countless lives by concluding – correctly – that cholera is a *water*-borne illness that has nothing to do with 'miasma'.

There's a price for hanging onto a bad idea. Sometimes it's your life. Sometimes it's someone else's. But when the tolls are tallied, *reality* rings them up.

Everything Changes All the Time

EVERYTHING CHANGES ALL THE TIME.

This is so and cannot be denied.

A rock was once a spoonful of something fluid, then a solidifying mass, then a segmented piece of mass, then an imperceptibly degrading portion of its previous incarnation.

A day begins with shades of light defining the horizon, then grows to full stature across a portion of the planet, then decays into darkness, which then is followed by yet another day.

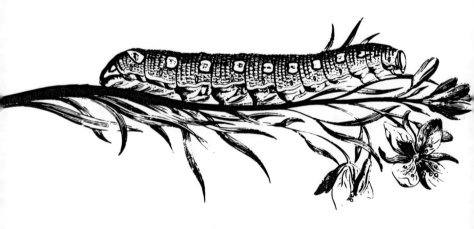

A baby is conceived, gestates, is born, slowly reaches maturity, has a baby of its own, and follows the sunset into old age, death, and decay.

All things change all the time. As comforting as it might be to say 'Stop!' and have all things remain as they are, that cannot be so. Time is change and cannot be delayed.

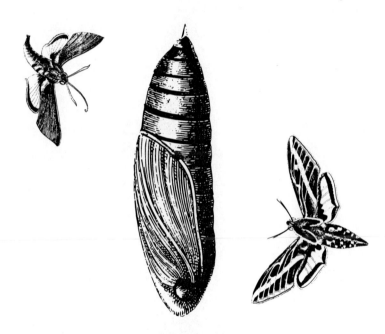

Or can you prevent *this* moment from becoming...*this* moment?

For the living, survival depends on adapting continuously to those moment-to-moment changes. Surviving is no small thing. It is the primal impulse of all the many species. Life, then, requires an ongoing adjustment to an endless series of challenges.

Over thousands and millions of years, species have evolved brilliant methods by which to enable their survival. Cheetahs run faster than their prey. Giraffes' long necks allow them to find food far out of the reach of their competitors. Microbes can withstand the intense heat and lack of light at the bottom of the ocean. One finch's beak is long and pointed for probing. Another finch cracks open its food with a shorter, stronger beak. They both have wings to carry them away from predators.

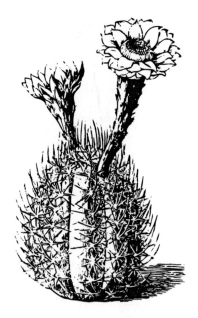

Plants have devised elegant, ingenious systems for the distribution of their seeds. Cattails and dandelions inseminate the breeze. Ground weeds attach burrs to the feet and fur of passing animals. Desert plants have learned to live on little water. High-mountain flowers spring from thin soil on top of rock.

Each of these and countless other species have
figured out a niche. That is, an advantage over their
environment that helps perpetuate the species.

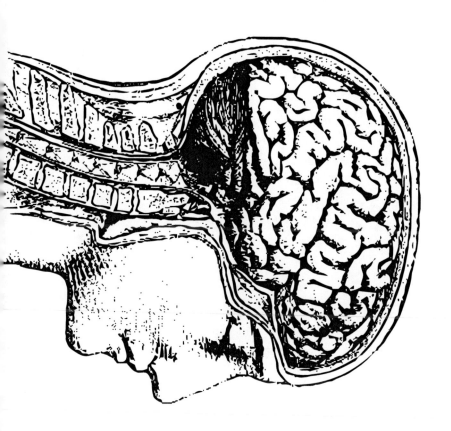

For humans, that advantage is the prefrontal
cortex of the brain – the advantage with which
we discovered the source of our advantage.

Shortcut

The way that we discover...
is the book and not the cover.
It's the fact and not the fiction,
the meaning, not the diction.
It's the tools and not the toys.
It is the signal, not the noise.

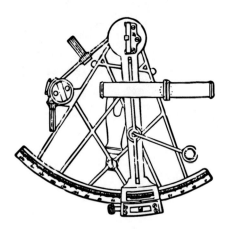

Up and In

MAGINE YOU'RE A PREHISTORIC PERSON, with hairy arms and hairy feet. Worried through the night about those cruel and crazy predators who do not care about your wants and needs, much less about your humble hopes and dreams. They just want to kill and eat you, not to take the time to *meet* you. And when their hunger comes again, they'd love to dine on your best friend.

That means you don't have time to think about the finer things in life. A good night's sleep would be a dream. Maybe four or five unconscious hours without a twig snap on the outer edge of earshot. *That* would be a good night's sleep.

An unthreatened meal would be a finer thing, too. Just a chance to gnaw on the raw flank of fresh-killed rabbit, perhaps. Shared with a mate or a child. Uninterrupted nutrition – not just for the sake of survival, but safe enough to *savor*. A tasty meal on a pleasant day, among one's ever-vulnerable family. No worries, for a moment, about large-pawed canines tiptoeing up through the weeds, with sights set on your loved ones, your meal, or *you*.

Yes, back in the days before fences and guns and houses with roofs. Back when *homo sapiens* were only just participants in a game that we were ill-equipped to win. Slower than our rivals. Weaker. More vulnerable to the elements. Producing babies that took too long to reach adulthood. Couldn't fly. Couldn't swim.

And now, here comes that pack of hungry wolves. And that ox they came to gore is *you*. And your mate. And oh yes, no less, your *children*, too.

As the wolves approach, you don't know why, but you throw a rock, and hit one in the eye. Maybe there's just nothing else that you could do. You may even be as startled as the wolf, who yelps and turns away. The other wolves exchange confusion. This is something they have never seen before! In the eon of evolution in which the wolf neared the apex of the food chain, no prey has ever pre-emptively inflicted pain upon this predator.

And as the mild and fearful *human*, you have never known anything but retreat from the lupine killing machine. But now, suddenly, something has changed. A wolf with ill intent is now more concerned about what you did to it than what *it* was about to do to *you*.

You quickly hurl another rock, which bounces off the head of another startled wolf. The pack knows something quirky has just occurred. This scrawny, wingless, slow-footed *two*-legged has delivered pain to *that* wolf and to *that* one.

In this moment of confusion, retreat seems like the obvious option. The wolves trot away to regroup. 'What the hell was *that*?' they wonder in the way that wolves may wonder.

The wolves are bright enough to respect the impact of the rocks just thrown. But not brighter. *You*, on the other hand, have just initiated a series of events that started with an instinct, followed by reaction, and which eventually begat sport, the game of baseball, the art of pitching, and the wonders of Satchel Paige himself, which include his 'step-n-pitch-it', his 'submariner', his 'sidearmer', and his 'bat dodger' pitches.

And the bean ball to the side of that wolf's head? Satchel might've called *that* one the 'evolver'.

A New Pair of Wings

BASEBALL IS A PLAYFUL DEMONSTRATION of the fun you can have with the laws of physics. But humans aren't the only species that can figure things out. It's often a game of life and death. If you win it, you live. If you lose it, you die.

It seems obvious that the driving desire of all forms of life is the perpetuation of the species. *Survival* is the fundamental goal. It wouldn't be hard to win that game if nothing ever changed. Whales would always find soothing water and plenty of krill to eat. Cheetahs would always outrun wildebeests.

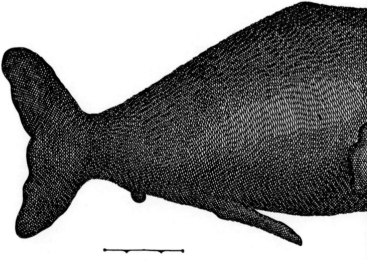

It's a great system if you're a whale or a cheetah. Not so good for the prey, whose conviction to continue is as dear as any other's. So all forms of life are designed, above all, as reproduction machines. That's why the sexual urge is so powerful. *Individuals* eventually die. Reproduction ensures that the *species* abides.

But while those urges never change, the external forces challenging each species change all the time. What worked yesterday won't necessarily work today. Improvisation is essential. Thanks to the cognitive power of our prefrontal cortices, we humans are able to make mental adjustments in real time. (We sometimes choose *not* to, which is a most regrettable side effect of consciousness.)

In the meantime, other species don't have the luxury of convincing themselves that reality is a choice. Take, for example, a species of birds known as cliff swallows. Over the millennia, they figured out that if they made nests out of mud, on vertical surfaces above the ground, below overhangs, they could reproduce beyond the reach of predators, and with some protection from the elements. It's a brilliant strategy.

Until it encountered humanity, on the sultry savanna of the state of Nebraska. In the early years of the nuclear era, an interstate highway was laid as a form of civil defense, through the fertile fields of corn. But as often happens, original intentions were replaced over time. Civil defense gave way to the simple convenience of unimpeded transportation.

The interstate highway became a conduit of commerce.
No intersections. No stop signs. Nothing to delay the
movement of massive vehicles fast across the land,
save bad weather and the occasional need to refuel.

To eliminate traffic-slowing crossroads, bridges were
built over the interstate highway – bridges with vertical
side walls and overhangs. In other words, suitable sites
for colonies of cliff swallows to incubate their families.

On the other wing, as you might imagine, two-ounce
birds don't stand much of a chance against the front
end of a 40-ton vehicle moving 80 miles an hour, mere
meters below their nests. It's a risky space for *adult* cliff
swallows to navigate, and an even riskier place in which
to teach their offspring to fly. It would be like learning
to swim in a storm-surging surf at Waimea Bay.

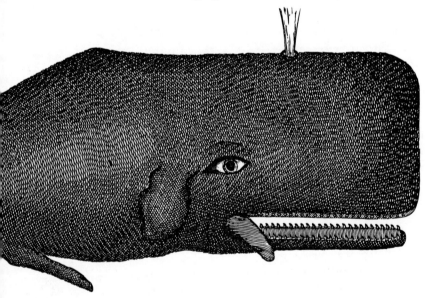

Scientists began to study the cliff swallows killed near

those interstate bridges. Over time, they discovered
that fewer swallows were being killed by the traffic
roaring beneath their nests. Oh, the traffic hadn't
decreased or slowed down. But something important
had changed in the 30 years since the study began
– the average length of the cliff swallows' wings.

The newer generations had *shorter* wings, which
enabled them to take off and gain altitude faster than
their longer-winged ancestors; shorter wings that
allowed them to live long enough to reproduce, and
to pass the shorter-wing genes on to their offspring.

Thus, cliff swallows had adapted to changing
circumstances, in order to survive. They figured out
how to win a new game within the laws of physics – no
matter how much they might have preferred the longer
wings that provided an advantage to their *ancestors*.

The newer generations of birds adapted to meet the
demands of the new reality in which they found
themselves. Because when you hear a rumbling mass of
deadly force headed in your direction, all the obstinacy,
culture, and tradition in the world won't save your life.

But a pair of those quick-launch wings
might send you home safely to your family,
without so much as a ruffled feather.

Amoeba and Me

Amoeba, amoeba,
so simple, but still –
so much to accomplish,
so much to fulfill!

Indeed, my amoeba,
the things that you do!
Divide by mitosis,
and then there are two.

I see, *mon* amoeba
your pseudopod feet
are weary from gathering
algae to eat.

¡*Arriba*, amoeba!
The more that I see,
the more your endeavors
remind me of me.

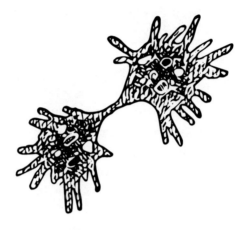

The Pine Cone Needs No Explanation

CHARLES DARWIN OBSERVED THAT 'Everything in nature is the result of fixed laws'. And all forms of life – but *one* – accept these inevitabilities. All forms, but *one*, are not equipped to doubt. They have no need to invent exceptions to these fixed laws.

A pine cone falls to the forest floor. Its further fate depends on circumstance – soil, sunshine, sufficient moisture. Many fall. A few take root. Some grow into trees and rise quietly to the sky.

None argue with the fixed laws. All abide. From seed to struggle to maturity to death, all *are*. No more, no less. All take, all give, according to the laws set forth. *How* the laws – not contemplated. *Why* the laws – not contemplated.

And yet the textures, complexities, and varieties are infinite. No perfume more sublime than the soft scent of a pine forest. No sound more soothing than wind through the trees.

No cathedral more holy. All simply *is*.

Man enters the forest preoccupied with intentions
and plans, which create an illusion of separation.
We think. We calculate. Therefore, we are
exceptional. (*We think.*) The fixed laws of
nature are subject to doubt, ridicule, repeal.
(*We think.*) What we decide is, *is*. (*We
think.*) What we decide is not, *is not*. (*We
think.*) Simply by deciding. Because unlike
every other form of life, we have the
ability *to choose* to *decide*. And so we do.

But reality is indifferent to our discretion.
A human may build a boat to skim
the seas, but no hull is immune to
the laws of buoyancy. A human may
decipher the principles of aeronautics
and learn to fly, but violations of those
principles will be enforced *immediately*.

No thought or effort is needed to deny
what is. Ask any fool. You will find that
reality has no mercy on the fool. But it
rewards all those who would honor and
accept it. And we humans who respectfully
seek to understand its divinely-ordained laws
may savor its flavors on a privileged level.

But the pine cone needs no explanation.
May we seek also to understand *that*.

The Noble and the Profane

CLIFF SWALLOWS HAVE THE ADVANTAGE of evolving without the distraction of irrational thought. This provides them a purity of purpose that can be a challenge for the human species. Without conscious thought, the path to survival is direct. Something either works, or you die. If enough individuals of your species die, your species dies off, too.

And yet extinction runs counter to the primal instincts of individuals and species. So adaptations that enhance survivability are embraced without question – at least among all species that do not have the capacity for conscious thought. For cliff swallows, the adoptation of shorter wings is good, because it helps the species to survive. There is no tradition-based insistence on the superiority of longer wings.

As far as we now know, humans are the exception among all the things that live, because of our ability to think self-reflectively. With that ability, we have accomplished wondrous things. Medicine, architecture, *haute cuisine*. Self-reflective thinking provides us the unique potential for *lucid evolution*. That is, the ability to evolve consciously, with purpose, in an ever-more enlightened direction.

But conscious thought comes with an unintended consequence. Along with the ability to make things better, is the ability to choose a path that *undermines* individual and collective survival. Now, how in the name of Charles Darwin can that possibly happen? You might call it a hardware failure or a bug in the program, but it relates to a vestige of the evolutionary process itself.

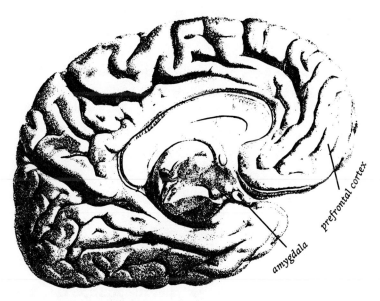

The prefrontal cortex that evolved in humans and which enables higher-order thinking did not *replace* the earlier iterations of our brains. Instead, it was *added on* to the previous versions, which still perform their original functions. At the core of all this is the amygdala, a component we share with such relatives in the animal kingdom as the lizard and the skunk. The amygdala is responsible for emotional responses like fear, anxiety, and aggression.

This means that our highly-evolved brains come with a built-in paradox: the noble and the profane share the same beleaguered skull. If the prefrontal cortex represents where we are and what we might become as a species, the amygdala represents where we came from.

The amygdala speaks with the voice that says, 'Me want!' Me want candy. Me want toy. Me want my way! The amygdala does not think, plan, create, or dream. Instead, it craves, fears, and reacts.

The amygdala fears the wolves in the night. The prefrontal cortex figures out how to build a fire.

The prefrontal cortex observes the movements of the celestial bodies, and figures out how they must therefore be organized. The amygdala imprisons the observer, because he undermines religious dogma.

The prefrontal cortex writes the Gettysburg Address. The amygdala murders Abraham Lincoln.

The prefrontal cortex investigates the principles of aerodynamics and invents the airplane. The amygdala persuades humans to kill themselves and slaughter thousands of innocent strangers by flying airplanes into buildings.

The prefrontal cortex enables scientists to successfully plan and complete a manned mission to the moon. The amygdala convinces a small but dementedlycertain group that the mission was a hoax.

Because of this quirk in our anatomy, we humans have the ability to convince ourselves that the *wrong* path is the *right* one, in spite of all evidence to the contrary.

An amygdala might save you from a shark attack, but it will not build you a boat. It is a fool who *chooses* not to know the difference.

Let us therefore investigate the ways in which we fool ourselves, so that we may cease to do so.

Humanity comes to terms with gravity

All the Theologians in Christendom

A PALEOLITHIC HIPSTER WANDERS INTO A CAVE. Being the creative type, he or she sees, not the walls of a cave in the flicking lamplight, but a *canvas* on which to make a statement.

We aren't sure what inspired the images of animals that were drawn upon those walls so compellingly. Maybe they were intended to bring luck to the hunters. Or to invoke the divine. Or to impress a potential mate. Or simply to record a particular reality of the Paleolithic hipster's life.

From whence came Banksy: Lascaux masterpiece speaks through time.

We may never know the original intent of those drawings. But they waited for 17,000 years in their darkened gallery, until one day, a young Frenchman named Marcel Ravidat found the way back into the cave. And although Marcel spoke a language that did not exist when the drawings were made, and the artist's language had long-since been lost, Marcel immediately recognized what he saw.

He understood the drawings as an artifact of human presence – a statement that we are on the scene, and we are processing our experience. Over time, the *symbolic* meaning decays and the value that remains is the beauty of the art.

Helios pulls a myth across the sky

We know more about the purpose of the Greek myth of Helios, who, as every day went by, drove the chariot of the Sun across the sky. The story was a way to explain what the science of the day could not, while evidence was still being gathered. It was a story told so well as to generate its own appeal, *separate* from the reality it was created to describe.

We value Helios' poetic imagery long after its practical purpose has expired. Meanwhile, we have learned that Copernicus' explanation of the Sun's behavior, though perhaps less *emotionally* appealing, is the more accurate description of *reality*.

And yet, from Beowulf to Bigfoot, we humans love a tall tale. Fictions and legends have their virtues – to amuse and entertain, to activate the imagination, and to bind cultures over time. When reality is less appealing, or too painful to confront, it's comforting to find refuge in a fairy tale. So the hobo dreams of the Big Rock Candy Mountain, 'where the hens lay soft-boiled eggs'. Wouldn't that be nice?

As an imaginary character once said, without a first or a second thought, 'When the legend becomes fact, print the legend.' And that's no sweat whatsoever, in an *imaginary* world. No one really suffers in the land of make believe, because no one breathes and no one bleeds in the land of make believe.

But it matters not how pleasant it would be 'to paddle all around in a big canoe, in a lake of stew, and of whiskey, too'. Outside of the hobo's hoping, there ain't no Candy Mountain.

To believe to this day that Helios actually pulls the Sun across the sky, is what is known as a *delusion*. That is, a lie told, not to someone else, but a lie one tells one's *self*.

Oh, the multitude of sorrows that are sired by delusion!

By that unique *homo sapien* capacity to insist that the myth is the reality; that the fiction is the fact. And from that act, behold...a brand new fool is born!

There are reasons why such foolishness persists upon the world. They include fear and ignorance, dishonesty and dogma, superstition and religion, cults, conformity, conspiracy theories, belief systems and patriotism, orthodoxies of all kinds, all pimped for profit by the malevolent patrons of power.

It doesn't matter to *reality* what people convince themselves is true. But it does matter.

Galileo was threatened with torture, and *imprisoned* by the Catholic Church, for speaking what proved to

be the truth about the relationship between Earth
and the Sun. He was imprisoned for threatening an
authority built on an *imaginary* explanation of what is.

But long after scientific instruments had validated,
again and again and again, the accuracy of Galileo's
explanation, and long after his ideas mapped out
realities that helped humanity to plan and execute a
trip to the moon, the Catholic Church remained silent.

Finally, in 1992 – *359 years* after his
death – the Catholic Church conceded
that in fact, Galileo had been correct.

In all that time, the Earth kept revolving around the
Sun. Day after day after day. The Sun didn't care
what the Greeks thought it was doing, or what the
Catholic Church thought it was doing, or even what
Galileo thought it was doing. It simply *was*. And *is*.

Others may win a prize, or a following, or a fortune,
for the most entertaining explanation of celestial
behavior. We might even say that one of those
other explanations is what celestial behavior *ought*
to be. But Copernicus and Galileo, and Aristarchus
of Samos before them, win the prize for using
their intellect to figure out what actually *is*.

The difference between what we *think* should be and
what *is*, can be profound. To know the difference,
and to get it right, is fundamental to our existence.
There's nothing wrong with embracing a fiction
for aesthetic reasons. Or to be entertained. But

it can be *fatal* to insist that myth or superstition represent reality, when in fact they do not.

The Greeks created an epic and compelling story, which doubled as a scientific explanation, until it didn't. Then it remained as an epic and compelling story that still tells us something about the ancient Greek civilization...but nothing about how the Sun behaves.

May we remain mindful that Galileo was not imprisoned for being wrong. And that all the theologians in Christendom couldn't make the Sun revolve around the Earth.

Parsimony

Oh, I've tried my share of razors;
Gillette and all the rest.
But when I crave a clean, close shave –
Occam's is the best!

Mind Traps

AVE YOU EVER BEEN CAUGHT IN A TRAP? You know, a place you get stuck in, and you want to get out, but you can't seem to figure out how? And the longer you're stuck there, the more you're aware that the trap wasn't set with your best interests in mind. Even worse is a trap that's so well-designed that you don't even know you've been trapped. Either way, what remains of your short time on Earth is no longer yours to determine.

Some traps you can touch, like a mouse trap. They keep whatever is trapped from moving to anywhere else.

Some traps you *can't* touch. They're *mind* traps. They lock down your mind so *it* can't move anywhere else.

Any kind of creature can get caught in a trap. But only a *human* can get caught in a mind trap. You see, a mind trap depends on the suspension of disbelief that can only occur in the gullible nethers of the feckless mind of a fool. Or of a generous soul too willing to hand out the benefit of a doubt.

A mind trap is constructed of untruths – fantasies, fallacies, delusions and/or lies – that someone convinces someone else to believe. When the untruth is *believed*, it turns into the trap. Oh, anyone who is trapped could *think* their way out of the trap, any time. They just don't realize that the only reason the trap exists is because they *believe* that it does.

But do not despair! Though the ages, mind stars – heroes of the human mind – have devised an ingenious system to avoid the mind traps, and thereby, to discover truth. The heroes include Ibn al-Haytham, Robert Grosseteste, Roger Bacon, William of Occam, Albertus Magnus, and Francis Bacon.

The scientific method they developed is based on the notion that truth is that which corresponds with *reality*, and that empirical evidence, reasoning, experimentation, logic, and mathematics help establish confidence in scientific conclusions. Knowledge is not a fixed place or a finish line, but a thrilling and unending journey toward destinations unknown.

By refining the map of the landscape of reality each step of the way, we travelers navigate ever-closer to the next port of call, and do not fall victim to the mind traps that lurk in tempting shadows.

There are tools that enable our pursuit of the truth. Our old friend Galileo incorporated one of the first telescopes in his scientific method, as he investigated celestial bodies. But although he was the first human to see spots on the Sun, and the moons around Jupiter, the mind trap he faced was twelve hundred years old. And the Catholic Church had not lasted that long by indulging blasphemers or demonstrable facts.

Had the purpose of the Church been a quest for
truth, it would have embraced Galileo's discoveries.
But the Church exists only to entrap human
minds, through tall tales and promises accepted on
faith, to ensure only the survival of the Church.

While Catholic dogma remains suspended in
the amber of antiquity, the scientific method
constantly re-calibrates its coordinates. Isaac
Newton, born in the year that Galileo died, made
further advances in our understanding of the
physical principles that govern our reality.

Albert Einstein refined Newton's work, and advanced
it further. Others have done the same with Einstein's.
*As Galileo, Newton, and Einstein would have expected
them to.* This is how the scientific method works.
Each participant moves our understanding closer to
the truth, and then the next one moves it closer.

The illusion of omniscience is a mind
trap of old. Ah, but the journey toward
enlightenment is a dance with the divine!

That Floating Feeling

A boat with a hole in the hull will sink. Not because of what I *think* it will do, or what I *want* it to do, but because it *will*. The principles of buoyancy do not care whether I do not want the boat to sink, or whether I think the boat will sink, or whether I think the boat will *not* sink. They are what they are. If they are honored, the boat will float. If they are ignored, the boat will sink.

The principles of buoyancy existed long before they were discovered by human beings. They are timeless and indifferent to human desires, human beliefs, and human awareness. But once they were unlocked by humans, those principles provided the framework by which people could travel over water. This led to the expansion of cultures, new

means of commerce, and a greater understanding
of other principles by which the world operates.

Knowledge begets knowledge. Driven by curiosity and
a unique intellectual capacity, humans have uncovered
many of the universe's underlying principles. Human
progress is indebted to our relentless deciphering of
the principles that represent the currents on which
life flows. And upon which a buoyant boat may float.

Natura Abhorret Doctrina

A doctrine (*aka* belief system, ideology, religion, theology, orthodoxy, sect, creed, dogma, academic construct, mind cage, mind trap, party line) is a closed-loop, human-contrived system of rules and beliefs that disables the ability of its victims to think freely or rationally, and/or to act in their own self-interest.

Doctrines cannot be questioned or debated, because they are not embraced on the basis of evidence or reason, but on faith and conviction alone.

The details of doctrines are less than the matter; their *effects* are in essence the same.

As viral parasites, doctrines exist to benefit *themselves*, not the host humans they infect to service their needs.

Doctrines are ultimately used as weapons of oppression against the uninfected.

Nature abhors a doctrine.

The Congregation of Learning

THE TRIUMPHS OF HUMAN PROGRESS SURROUND US. They're so common that it's easy to believe they were simply bequeathed to us with this green and pleasant Earth itself. Controllable fire. Agriculture. The wheel. Woven fabric. Navigation. Roads. Paint. Paper. Literacy. Books. Music. Buildings. Government. Water distribution. Geology. Biology. Controllable electricity. Movies. Television. Computers. Space travel. Cell phones. Buttered toast. *Café au lait.*

We accept these conveniences as irreplaceable parts of our lives, often without awaring that each represents the latest result of a series of insights and understandings figured out over time and toil, by fellow human beings. Each advance of knowledge by one human was further advanced by another, so that all humans may benefit from this congregation of learning.

It is by means of this congregation that humans as a species may inhabit all corners of the Earth, and communicate as fast as the speed of sound and light allow. It is by means of this congregation that we may overcome medical challenges that, before, had harmed countless among us, without mercy.

It is by means of this congregation that we may continue to live, in some degree of civilization, with billions of fellow humans.

The landscape of human achievement is breathtaking. But there are limits to our achievements. Many of those limits are self-imposed – and all of the self-imposed limits are needless. They can, however, be conquered by learning. This exceptional ability to learn is the capacity that distinguishes humans from all the forms of life that we now know.

This ability comes easily to some, and lies dormant or unknown to others. But it is available to all, and it is available throughout each life. Learning is a continuous process that is mastered with continuous, life-long practice. And the immeasurable *rewards* of learning? Life-long and continuous!

Socrates, a Visionary Head
– drawn by William Blake

The Thinkers and the Tinkerers

Did superstition conquer polio?
I do not think it did.
Scientific method, though,
found the causes that were hid.

And human presence in the sky,
conceived at Kitty Hawk,
resulted from experiments,
and not from groundless talk.

Belief is not a process
or path to enlightenment.
On faith we place our hope-filled bets,
then wonder where the money went.

The thinkers and the tinkerers
and the ones who take the chances
discover what has hindered us,
that we may make advances.

Puzzlementation

ONTINUOUS LEARNERS ARE CURIOUS. They wonder what makes some things work, and other things *not* work. They observe themselves and the world around them. Their approach to life can be summed up simply as, 'Figure things out and make things better!'

Why do they bother? Because it is fun! It is in fact its own reward! Have you ever worked on a jigsaw puzzle? Or solved a puzzle of any kind? Our minds are evolved to embrace a challenge. It can be more challenging to walk past a table covered with jigsaw pieces and *not* stop long enough to fit a few of the pieces together. 'Can you do it?' they seem to ask. 'Can you solve this simple task?'

So you evaluate the shapes of the available pieces, and in your mind you test the complementary patterns on their edges. You develop a 'theory' that a particular pair of pieces might be the pair that fits together. Then you test your theory by trying to connect them. If they snap together...*Eureka!* You met a little challenge and you exercised your mind, for which your mind rewards itself with a sip of fresh endorphins.

And if the pieces do *not* fit? Then you have a new decision – do you give up, or do you try again? You might quit because you're out of time. Other duties call! Go, go, go – you've got a busy life to live! Too busy to waste time on some random little puzzle. But if leave you must, then you must leave with a lingering sense of *pleasure unfulfilled*. That random little puzzle presented its inscrutable challenge, which you engaged...and then you walked away from.

On the other hand, you might have a few more minutes left to spend, or a competitive streak you must indulge. Those two pieces you tried to fit were close, but they were not the perfect fit. You decide to try again. But now you have a slight advantage that you didn't have before. Now you know a possible combination of pieces that *isn't* the correct one. Your chances of success are thereby now improved.

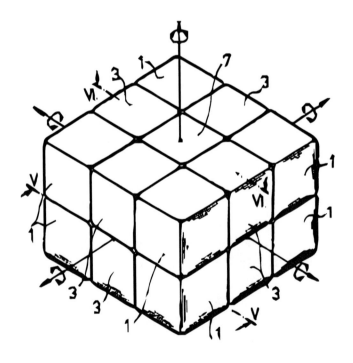

You find a new potential pair and then you try again. *They fit!* And because it took you twice the tries, your reward is even greater than it would have been the first time. The greater is the challenge, you note, the greater the reward. And if it took a third try or a fourth try before succeeding, you would find your satisfaction grew in proportional degrees.

But let's say you'd simply sauntered past that table, glanced down and quickly found two pieces that fit properly together, and then you'd kept on walking. Even *then*, in that successful moment, you would have earned a greater satisfaction than if you had not bothered to even shift your eyes toward the puzzle. That's just the way that we are wired.

All of life, as it passes by, presents us with a challenge – a puzzle to be solved. Then it presents us with another. And another. And another. As I contemplate the words to write within this sentence. And now, the words in *this* one. And a hundred other challenges that I must meet today. And I find the more elegantly I meet each one, the more gracefully I live. And the more that I ignore them, the more I struggle to get by.

Each challenge that confronts me is a decision I must make: 'I choose not to understand.' or, 'I will figure this one out.' The first choice brings me sorrow, for there is no joy in ignorance. But the second choice sends me soaring. So I resolve to practice on the latter path, that I might find the finest portrait that emerges from the puzzle of my life.

May, remain!

May, remain another day!
Stick around – don't go away.
Impatient life came out to play,
and we have so much more to say.
Oh, May, remain another day!
I beg of thee – don't go away!

BULLSHIT DOESN'T AGE WELL.

The Agents of Endarkenment

How on Earth did we lose our way,
with minds designed to find the light?
We lost our way, we lost our *minds*
to the agents of endarkenment.

No matter what our eyes behold,
we've trusted in the lies they sold.
We gave up sensibility, and bought
their cost-free path to bankruptcy.

No cost at all *in thought*, that is.
Only the full value of our *souls*.
To ensure that we remain confined,
and voluntarily blind,
until our options have expired,
and our speedy lease on life, retired.

'Why, *I would just do* anything
to hear those soothing words again.
And let some confident authority
forever take control of me.
I get a little tingle,
and I never doubt a single thing
big daddy ever yells at me.
And he will make sure all is right,
so I will need not fear or flight
the dreadful things that fill the night.'

Oh, the agents of endarkenment!
They steal the light from every eye,
they lie, they lie, they lie, they *lie*,
they lie until the day we die.

And all we have to do is buy their lie;
they barely even have to *try*.
'The sky is down, the ground's the sky,'
and we don't ever ask them 'Why?'

This is how we lost our way,
we gave our precious minds away.
To thieves and soothing psychopaths –
weeds that conceal the beatin' path.

May I Offer You A Lie?

May I offer you a lie –
in exchange for which, your life?
It's the finest lie that you will hear;
a lie that conquers every fear.

And if this lie were only true,
there'd be nothing else for you to do.
For, in its theoretic way,
it might warm the coldest day.

No actual meal might taste as good
as this imaginary food.
Why struggle for prosperity?
Why indulge reality?

I guarantee you will not find
a more satisfying lie than mine.
You'll never need another lie,
so don't let this lie pass you by!

The Dirty Work

 OU HAVE A NEED. I HAVE A SOLUTION. Let's do some business. Water? Yes, of course. You and your wife and the baby and the boy, that's a lot of overhead. You won't make it across the valley without water. There's no water out there. Scorpions, maybe a heat-crazy snake or two, but no *water*. Life is the question, right? No water, no life.

I won't lie to you. It's not easy, even if you have water. That sun is hot. It's so hot those men with guns that you say are coming after you, they won't go out there in the middle of the day. So the Sun is your friend. The men with guns will kill you if they catch you. The woman, the boy, and the baby, too. You know that. Those men have orders. But they're not suicidal. They won't go out there on a day like this.

That brings us back to my canvas bag. What you need is water, my friend. We make a deal. Your gun for this water. Once you make it across the valley, you won't need the gun. Those are friendly people over there. You know that. I would give you the water if I could, but there isn't any to spare. That's one reason the men with guns won't go out there in the sun. Water rations are too small.

Hey, that's a cute baby! You must be an optimist to

bring a baby into a world like this. It takes an optimist these days, *n'est-ce pas?* Hope springs eternal! This bag holds two liters. Just enough to get you there. You don't want to waste it! The boy, he looks like he wants a drink right now, but be careful! Little sips.

You ever seen a canvas water bag before? Old school. Very old school. Simple, but effective. See, it looks like it's leaking, but that's not a leak. It's evaporation. Keeps the water cool. Helps seal the canvas. It seems inside out, but it's not. Ingenious design. You want that moisture on the outside.

To tell you the truth, I hate to let this water go. You know how scarce it is around here. You are fortunate to have something valuable enough for me to even *consider* making this exchange. But you have a need, and let's be honest here. I'm in business to do business. A gun has value. You have a serious gun. If it wasn't for the woman and children, you could probably defend yourself quite successfully with this gun. The men behind you don't have anything nearly as deadly.

But of course you would not want to expose a small
family to the crossfire. Only a fool would do that.

But you must decide quickly, *amigo*. If those men
are that close behind, and they catch up with you
here, the outcome would not be good. You take this
water, in exchange for the gun. Then go, yes? Protect
your family. Lead them to safety across the valley.

We have a deal? Very good, very good!
Farewell! Remember, sip slowly. Don't
waste a drop! You can make it...

Such a gun. I must hide it before the men with guns arrive!

With the woman and the two young children? Yes,
yes I saw the man. They were here, maybe an hour
ago. They set out across the valley. I gave them some
water. Wait, wait! Don't shoot! Listen to me! They
won't make it! The water bag leaks! I convinced him
it was not a leak. He believed me. He was desperate.
Look at the sun! They won't make it halfway across
the valley. Save your bullets. Save your water. You
can find their bodies out there tonight, after the
sand cools. Let nature do the dirty work, eh?

The Abuse of Truth

GEORGE ORWELL WROTE A MASTERPIECE about the abuse of truth, called 1984. In it, the agents of oppression understood that if they could persuade a free-thinking human that what was *not* true, *was* true, then they would obtain absolute power over that individual. They also understood that all of their corrupt purposes would be threatened if even *one person* held out for the truth.

...and George Orwell is watching Big Brother.

They used a simple equation to measure their powers
of coercion. (That is, to measure their ability, through
any means necessary, to convince an individual
that even the most obvious falsehood was *true*.)

The oppressors in Orwell's Oceania were personified
by O'Brien. O'Brien knew that once an individual
was willing to *believe* that 2 + 2 = 5, then that
person's soul had surrendered to obedient servitude.
And that Oceania's ability to conduct any form of
horror it could conceive need fear no challenge.

$$2 + 2 = \text{☠}$$

Therefore, *truth* was the *only* existential threat to the
fascists who controlled Oceania. Winston Smith, the
protagonist of 1984, was harder to persuade than
most of his fellow citizens. O'Brien went so far as to
lock a live rat in a cage around Smith's head, in his
effort to compromise Smith's commitment to truth.

O'Brien's ultimate role was *Enforcer of Lies*.

There are many tools in a liar's tool box. Sometimes it's
a seductive smile. Other times, it's torture. One uses
what one needs for the job at hand. But the purpose
of the tools is the same – for one party to obtain
advantage over another, by convincing the victim that
what is *not* true...*is*, and that what *is* true...*is not*.

The perpetrator of a lie knows the truth, but

deliberately chooses to misrepresent it, to gain advantage. As such, a lie is a fundamental act of hostility committed toward another human being.

A lie undermines the presumption of good faith on which society *relies*. It imposes upon the lied-to the burden of detecting the lie, then calibrating the distance between reality and the lie, and then *compensating* for the gap. Or worst of all, if the lie is believed, then the victim proceeds on a course that is in conflict with the truth. The original lie thus compounds itself and multiplies, forcing the victim into a hopeless battle against reality itself.

Meanwhile, survival depends on one's ability to acquire accurate information about immediate conditions, to determine the most appropriate response, and then to make whatever adjustments are needed to ensure the most favorable outcome. So if the *information* is not correct, the *adjustment* will not be correct. A lie therefore undermines another's ability to survive.

If you accept that the golden rule – *Do unto others as you would have them do unto you.* – is humanity's fundamental moral principle, then it follows that *every human has a basic right to the truth.*

The challenge, then, is to detect the dishonest agents like O'Brien who lurk among us, to protect ourselves against them, and at all times, to honor and discover the truth. For *truth* reveals the beatin' path.

A lie is told when reality does not align with what one *wishes* it to be. A lie may temporarily alter one's *perception* of reality, but it does not change reality.

A Little Lie

I told a little lie,
and here's the reason why:
I thought that I could slip it by,
and that in fact I could deny
I'd told a little lie.

It made some people high –
my tiny little lie.
Oh me, oh me, oh me, oh my!
I thought that it would pass right by,
that it would give me wings to fly.

Instead, my lie made people die.
Their mothers and their children cry,
and now I need an alibi.
Oh me, oh me, oh me, oh my...
I'll have to try another lie!

There's no such thing

as a good liar.

The Monster and the Fool

'1 + 1 is 3,'
 said the monster to the fool.
'Your friends and family
 all agree.'

The fool feared that if he disagreed,
he would have no friends or family.
But more, *much* more than that,
he feared the thought of *thinking*.

The monster did not threaten.
He knew he did not have to.
For more than anything at all,
the fool desired to fit in.
Not fitting in would be the torture,
threatened silently.

The fool was not inclined
to count the fingers on his hand.
Who cares about a number?
Certainly not the fool!

'How much is 1 + 1?'
 the monster asked,
 after another moment passed.

Even the fool could calculate
the easiest way to make some hay.
'1 + 1 is 3!' declared the fool.

This made the monster smile.
And then the fool smiled, too.
He loved the monster ever after!

Are You Who You Were?

Are you who you were then?
Or rather, do you *tell yourself*
that you are who you were then?

Most surely, you are *not*,
and could not ever be.
Except for then,
which is not now, and
nevermore will be again.

Instead, your discontent desire
marks you
like the reconstructed lips
of a starlet suing time.
The more that you resist,
the more that you *insist*.

Do not mistake our silence
for a share in your delusion.
We are merely too polite
to note the bogey
on your nose.
It is not a rose.
How sad it is to see you
act as if it was.

Or did you think that time
exempted you?
Or that reality invested
in what you *expected*
it would do?

Counting (on) My Delusions

How do I delude me?
Let me count the ways...
I'll always be just 23,
for a year's 10,000 days.

My hair grows thicker all the time,
on my head, and not my ears.
I get sober when I drink more wine,
I lose weight when I drink beer.

Time is on my side, my friends –
am I not younger every day?
I find the laughter never ends;
all expenses on this trip are paid.

Ignorance is strength, you see?
My sins are all excused.
My imagination pleases *me*,
if not the truth that I abuse.

If I run a little faster,
it might not catch up with me.
Delusion, be my master!
Let one plus one be three!

The Hopeless Hope

The weight of every second,
in existential battle with what *is*...
endlessly inventing explanations
of why the things that are not, *are*...
a permanent commitment
to the work of self-deception,
in which the ascent
of every moment's mountain
must be followed by another,
and another,
and another,
and another.
And every tick that passes by
demands the construct of another lie
to sustain the fragile
house of cards
that reaches
to the
s
k
y
.

A penny
for the fool
who must somehow
hold the balance,
while pirouetting past
each obstacle of truth,
with ears covered
and eyes closed,
in a breeze propelling those
who sail –
a breeze that has no mercy
on a life of lies
built edge on edge
in the hope-
less hope
that breeze will
never whisper
to the
atmosphere
a
g
a
i
n
.
.
.

Reality Always Wins

ROTHERS AND SISTERS, I SAY UNTO YOU, 'Behold the Sun, which riseth in the west and setteth daily in the east, and always has and thus it always shall, for this is Truth itself I sayeth unto thee!'

Tell me this. Is it then, true? Did what is *become* what is because I *say* it is? Or because *you* say it is? Or because he, or she, or it, or *they* say it is? Does the saying so *make* it so? If so, says who?

If you believe with great conviction that the Earth revolves the other way, you may believe so with more conviction than any person ever, about any thing that ever was. Does that then make it so?

And if you believe with such conviction that you convince him and her and all of us, that what you say is true? If you, in fact, persuade every living conscious soul on this abundant planet that east is west and west is east – is it therefore *so*?

Does belief create reality? Why, so it seems, in the minds of many here among us.

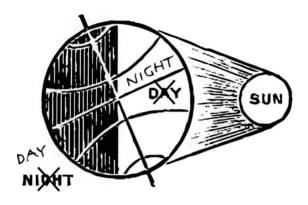

And what a wondrous triumph this has wrought – the special species that has learned to think – *decides* that what is...*is not*, and *decides* what is not...*is*. All hail the power of the simple human thought, as it commands the firmament! Is there anything humanity cannot manifest, simply by the act of *believing* it is *so*?

Alas, I think, there is. It should sadden me to say so, because I understand how satisfying it is to believe that belief itself can conquer all. And yet, what an arrogant delusion, wondrous though we are! But born of woman and at this moment, one and all mark time until starvation, disease, injury, or the inevitable entropy of old age ends our lucky trip through life. And in between we fart and shit and blow our noses, but somehow convince ourselves that *we* might deign to write the rules of life!

For a consequence of consciousness must surely be the ease with which we may reject, or just ignore, *what is*. What, after all, arrives with less effort than the lie or the self-deception? No calorie is burned. No insight is earned. No value is added. No light is shone.

It may feel good to think that sand is gold, and therefore, that you are rich. But sand is sand, and to act on the conviction that it is not, is to star as yourself in a movie called 'The Fool'. It is to disrespect reality itself. And *that*, no matter if it pleases you or not, is a sucker bet on a losing hand. Make no mistake, my friend – reality always wins.

I Met a Fool

Upon the path, I met a fool
untroubled by uncertainty.
'I never have to think, you see –
it's all been figured out for me.'

I warned him that bridge ahead
had washed out in the recent rain,
but his direction did not change.
He said, 'I'll cross it on my way again.'

I did not hear the fellow fall
into the chasm far below.
His reaction time was much too slow;
too many things he would not know.

I met another fool one day,
whose map still showed the bridge ahead.
'That bridge has washed away,' I said,
but now, alas, she too is dead.

Perhaps they both died happily,
confounded by their certainty.
But there remains the probability
of deaths, and lives, neither one could see.

Am I *this*, or am I *that?*

Nope.

A Thwart Upon His Nose

EHOLD THE BILLY BOY WHO DID NOT LIKE the things he saw. He did not like them one little bit! He did not want the world to change, and he always got the things he wanted.

So one day he declared that time itself would stop. And for what reason should he not? He was born of wealth, and as with so many of those who are, he mistook good fortune for something he had earned. And even more mistakenly, he mistook good fortune for something he *deserved*.

Now, Billy Boy was well-educated and well-traveled at a time when others suffered deeply from the Great Depression of the 1930s. But instead of gratitude and humility, Billy Boy believed himself somehow *entitled* to the advantages he inherited, through no ability or effort beyond the good fortune of his birth.

When all of one's needs are assured for the full duration of one's life, it is perhaps inevitable that *new needs* must be discovered. It is also perhaps inevitable that maturity is not a side effect of unlimited affluence. Most clearly it was not, in the case of Billy Boy.

When all the ponies and all the new toys around the world would not suffice, Billy Boy decided that what he needed most of all was for the world itself to change.

Can you make the world stand still, Billy Boy, Billy Boy?

Or more specifically, he needed the
world to *cease* its change.

At the cranky age of 30, little Billy Boy converted
petulance to a business plan and started a
magazine so that he could be boss of the world.
Do not laugh. At the time, young Billy Boy set
humility aside and pronounced that his new
magazine 'stands athwart history, yelling Stop, at
a time when no one is inclined to do so, or to
have much patience with those who so urge it'.

You see, no grownup would tell Billy Boy what he
could or could not do! If Billy Boy yelled 'Stop!',
the space/time continuum would stop, because
Billy Boy told it to. You're not the boss of Billy
Boy...and neither is space/time! Hubris hadth no
avatar more impeccably cast than Billy Boy.

But as George Orwell so vividly illustrated in 1984, if
one is willing to accept a single untrue assertion as
true, then one is capable of believing *anything*. And
in that moment, one surrenders unconditionally to
the malevolent intentions of the nearest authority.

There are people who are happy, without a
second thought, to proxy their minds to a dogma,
a belief system, an orthodoxy, a group, or to
someone else who wants control. 'It's easier than
thinking', they would think, if ever they took
the time to think. It allows them to feel a part of
something bigger. It provides the comfort of social
acceptance, for the simple price of mindlessness.

But ignorance is never a virtue, even when it is
disguised as the word of God. Or of a self-entitled
child. $2 + 2 \neq 5$, regardless of how desperately one
believes it does. In fact, to believe that it *could* is
to compromise one's ability to survive, and others'
ability to survive, as well. It is to set sail with one's
family in a boat with a hole in the hull, based on the
conviction that the laws of buoyancy do not exist. Or
do not apply. Or do not mean the difference between
survival on the water and death below the surface.

Reality found a patch of shade and doodled patiently
as Billy Boy and many of his fellow travelers grew old
and died. Stand athwart history and yell 'Stop', indeed!
Never was a notion more doomed upon conception. But
as we see, the persistence of ignorance strikes again
and again. Because Billy Boy's *idea does* live on, in
the hearts of those who so love a delusion, that they
give their only begotten minds, so that whosoever
believeth in his nonsense shall never have to think.

And yet, had Billy Boy successfully thwarted
history, he would remain alive to read these
words...which would never have been written.

Clueless and Cocky

I won't waste a minute on 'logic',
and 'reason' is never in season.
I'll say it again – the answer is '*Ten!*'
What was the question, again?

I'm clueless, but I am cocky.
It feels pure to be so sure!
Figure it out – there's no room for doubt
in a head full of cow manure.

You Have Two Choices

To one of two places
your choices will bring –
respect ye the truth,
or respect not a thing.

Ignorance Will Not Be Ignored

Ignorance is not benign.
At best, it drags its victim through a
sorrow-filled life of stupor.
At worst, it kills the host
that it infects.
Sometimes death comes quickly.

More often, death by
ignorance is an excruciating tour of hell,
in which even the most enlightened
of souls nearby are conscripted
into the horror.

The end comes never soon enough
to the ignorant,
or to the innocent,
who must suffer in their wake.

Ignorance is the enemy.

Grinning Inhofe Befouls the Habitat

GRINNING INHOFE MAKES HIS LIVING pimping lies for profit. His profit, not yours or mine. He even wrote a book of lies. Grinning Inhofe made profit on the lies within the book and upon the book itself. Grinning Inhofe values profit over truth, and profit over life.

The lies that Grinning Inhofe pimps are not the white ones that one might tell to save the self-respect of someone who may just have spilled her tea. No, the lies that Grinning Inhofe pimps will cause the deaths of you and me. Or, perhaps, of our posterity.

He lies about reality, he lies about the facts. He lies about the future and he lies about the past. Grinning Inhofe is a lie machine. Grinning Inhofe makes the world unclean.

Grinning Inhofe is a carrier, you see. He carries a disease called mendacity. He perpetrates dishonesty that threatens all the habitat. The habitat of all that lives, and as far as we now know, the only habitat in which all the living things will *ever* grow.

Grinning Inhofe will not suffer. He will not live

long enough to experience the full measure of his
lies. Not that his mendacity would allow him to
acknowledge the tempests and the hellish flames
of sorrow he sews so casually. Grinning Inhofe
will live out his life with ease, rewarded well by
those who profit much more than even he.

They know that Grinning Inhofe can be counted on to
pimp. And though he may be gone before you read this,
you may be sure the misery he pimped is near to you,
indeed. And that Grinning Inhofe would not care at
all; he was paid quite well for spoiling the habitat, and
for the sorrow that was  harvested from all of that.

Even Grinning Inhofe's grin is a lie.

Caveat Emptor

ONFIDENCE OR 'CON' ARTISTS HAVE SEPARATED SUCKERS from their valuables since the first two made acquaintance. Health tonics, real estate investments, Nigerian internet lottery scams – as long as there are people, some of them will be naive enough to forfeit their fortunes to a persuasive acquaintance who promises a non-existent payoff.

A con game requires at least two participants. First, a person with a personality and an offer so *believable*-seeming that they inspire 'confidence' in the mind of another person.

Second, another person, who is willing to invest money or some other valuable, based on good faith in the *word* of the person with the promise. Look closely, and you will see that the *credibility* of the first person is the *only* collateral offered.

In the Dark Ages, people sold random bones as the bones of saints, and splinters, as wood from the cross on which Jesus was crucified. There was, of course, no way to prove the claims, but a con artist could easily exploit the ignorance or desperation of a devotee well enough to make a sale. Details add believability to a con.

'This bone, from the third finger of the right hand of St. Paul, was given to a monk in Constantinople in 433 AD, where it was kept in the altar of a church, until the church burned down, 27 years ago. It was given to my father, a tradesman, in exchange for his help rebuilding the church. It has remained in my family ever since. Indeed, it is our most precious possession. But my older brother has taken on debt that he cannot otherwise repay, and in order to preserve what is left of our comfort and dignity, I am forced to sell this most precious artifact, from the very hand of St. Paul himself.'

To a believer with more money than sense, the chance to possess something so closely connected to the Lord & Savior must have seemed like the greatest of good fortune. Perhaps the bone was kept in a suitably ornamented pouch, or box.

But aside from those impressive words sent forth
from the seller's mouth, the buyer had no way
of knowing that the bone did not come from the
hand of a petty thief, dug up in a potter's field.

Honest people believe; dishonest people deceive.
And wise people demand to see the proof.

Had the buyer insisted on stronger evidence, there
never would have been a sale. The seller would have
moved on, until finding a buyer less skeptical of
the con. Of which there were many. And still are.

The success of the religious relic con – like any
con – depends on the conviction with which the
victim believes the lie on which it is based. In the
best of cons, that conviction is absolute; an article of
faith. That's why the victims are called 'believers'.

One might argue that a con is a victimless crime
in which both parties are complicit. But although
ignorance and despair provide the fertile ground,
deceit is the criminal seed. The damage from
such deceit is sometimes limited to an individual,
though that is more than damage enough. But
sometimes, it results in unspeakable miseries for
millions, as was witnessed in the Holocaust.

Let us take note that such deceit is a
preventable crime, and that devotion to *truth*
is the most effective weapon against it.

In the meantime, let us not forget that warning, coined

in the era of the holy relic racket: *Caveat emptor.* You may have heard it. It means, 'Let the buyer beware.'

Lest ye be played for a *foole*, that is!

Two Realms

I DO SO BELIEVE THAT I SHOULD BE boss
of the world, and that others should do what
I say, at all times of day. And that I could do
anything I want to do, and no one could stop me,
or make me do that which I do not want to.

I'd sleep all day if I felt that way. And if I went
to the beach to spend time with my friends, then
everyone else would be required to leave. I'd walk
into a store and take what I wanted, for free. I'd
throw trash on the ground and make someone
else pick it up, not *me*. I'd promise that I would do
something, then I'd deny that I ever said anything.

If I needed help from someone who didn't feel like
helping, I could still make them do it. I could say I
would *pay* them, and after they did what I paid them
to do, I would pay them with ten pounds of *nothing*. I
could have my way with someone's wife, and if she got
pregnant, I could make someone *else* raise the child.

If someone was suffering, I could steal all their
medicine. Or sell them some pills that I knew wouldn't
work. I could start horrid wars, and take prisoners
to torture and hold without charge...for as long as I
wanted. And then walk away; just go get my golf clubs
and *play*. Maybe dabble in painting. Spend time with

my grandkids. All those who displeased me would
never be seen! If I felt so inclined. *Anything.* And no
one could stop me, if I was the boss. I'd like that a *lot.*

...*wait!* Did I just hear you say something? Did you
just say that *you* should be boss of the world? What
a terrible thing that would be, since you are not *me!*
Incompatible, in fact, with *my* plans and desires.
That is why I should be boss of the world, not you.

And I *can* be, I guess, in the world of my mind.
There's nothing at all that I *can't* be, in there. But
you tell me that *you* are in charge of the world in
your mind. Outside of which, I am still free to be *me.*
As you are still free to be *you, outside* of the world

of *my* mind. Which leaves us in kind of a bind.

From which I can think of a *single* way out. And that
is that you rule the realm, from *your* skin, to within.
And I rule mine too, from *my* skin, to within. So
does everyone else who is born. But *outside* of our
skin, we're too many to live within worlds of our
own, are we not? For, who *chooses* to live by their
labor alone, independent of all? One in ten million,
perhaps? While the rest of us choose to cooperate,
in ways that allow us to peacefully share all the
space that exists from one's skin to another's.

We thereby surrender some boss-of-the-world
autonomy, to cohabit in *common* with others, even with
people we may never know. And the *personal* realm,
from the skin to within, remains our kingdom alone.

Therefore, we live in *two* realms – our own, and the
one that we share with all others – all the people, the
plants, fellow animals, and indeed, all the forms of life
that are yet to be met. And for *each*, our investment
in the state of the here and the now is *absolute*. And
your right to *your* world, ends at your skin. As *mine*
does at *mine*. And all in between is *equally ours*.

This sounds like a simple solution to a vexing concern,
does it not? And it is. Until someone decides that *they*
should be able to tell *me* what to do, or *you* what to do,
what to think, how to be, from our skin to within. They
may claim special power, special knowledge, or special
rights to impose *their* definitions on you and on me.

But when someone inserts their hand in
your pocket, your mind, your soul, or your
inalienable rights, you can be sure that their
purpose is not to enrich *your* place on Earth.

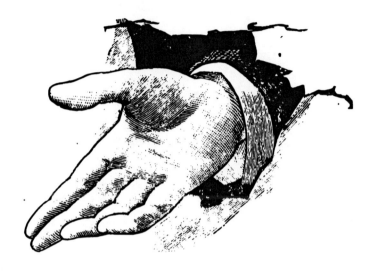

So if someone inserts their hand in your pocket,
your mind, your soul, or your inalienable rights,
make sure they withdraw a hand that is *empty*.

And if they insert it again, then make
sure that you hand back a *stump*.

This Time Among Us

E ARE BUSY, WE ARE BUSY, making many, many plans. Busy slipping in and out of our private/public places.

We are alone with our thoughts, alone with our beliefs, together with others who share our beliefs, and together with strangers whose beliefs we do not know. We are together here with our countrymen, together in a different country with others whose assumptions we may not hold in common, or even understand. Alone in private, alone in public, together with unseen others in our solitude.

These are *my* ways, those are *yours*. *These* we share, and *those* we don't, and little lambs eat ivy.

I end at my skin, and you end at yours, and in between us, all is *ours*. How do we play, and what are the rules of that common realm we are obliged to

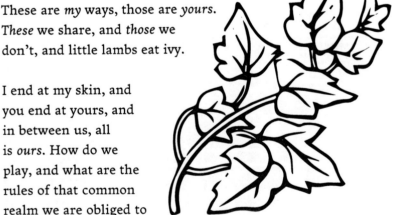

share? For all in creation must have their fair share.
A little for you, a little for me, some for the mouse,
and some for the bee. Equilibrium, you see, is no
triviality. I depend on you and you depend on me.

Or did you think that you were in this all alone?
Exceptional? Special? *Entitled*, perhaps, to all that you
find? On what then did you dine today? How came it to
your table? And just how is it that you happened to be
reading of these words? All by yourself, you individual,
you? Methinks you may have had a little help.

Don't get me wrong. I see you there – you, who are
uniquely you! And I count on you to help me see
the things *my* eyesight cannot see, as we count on
all the people who have taught us how to count.

Therefore, your reliability is most significant to
me. Give me your best, and do not deceive. *That*
is the key, the point of the balance, the substance
of all trust. Good faith must be given; good faith
must be received. I earn my place by sharing the
best eyes and ears and voice that I can muster. You
earn your place the same way. In the interest of
all, and of this moment in time we all share.

Trade Winds

You may surround yourself with surf,
upon an island far away.
But save your sense of isolation
for another day.

For although I might prefer
to think my fart offends no one,
I often find it *does*.
Or that my fart
is not a fart at all;
indeed, I am often told it *is*.
And my firmest belief to the contrary
seems to transfer
not the slightest conviction
to the noses of those around me.

It is neither what I *believe* it is,
nor of no interest to others
who are not me.
Once released, my fart
belongs to all downwind –
whose pleasure taken from it
is inversely less than mine
in dispatching it.
No matter how deeply it may have pleased *me*,
I have yet to be thanked for a fart.

I have therefore resolved
to be mindful of my farts,

in respect to the offense
they may cause to others.
Because, you see, neither one of us
are islands in the sea,
nor are the winds that
sully forth from thee,
or the winds that
sully forth from me.

A *belief system*
is a fixed view
of a reality
that always
changes.

I Know Why the Caged Mind Dies

PAUL LAURENCE DUNBAR KNOWS
THIS ABOUT BIRDS IN CAGES:

> I know why the caged bird sings, ah me,
> When his wing is bruised and his bosom sore,
> When he beats his bars and would be free;
> It is not a carol of joy or glee,
> But a prayer that he sends from his heart's deep core,
> But a plea, that upward to Heaven he flings –
> I know why the caged bird sings.

But why, oh why, is the caged bird *caged*?

To begin, it seems, because someone figured out how
to cage the bird. And then carried out the plan. And
maybe it amused him, or maybe it ornamented her
home, or eventually her hat. And then caging birds
became popular, and one of those things that people did
because it was one of those things that people did. Just
another unexamined permutation of life as it is lived.
As with clothing over genitals, roof above house, fire in
hearth, rug upon floor...bird within cage. Who knows
exactly when this came to pass, who knows exactly why?

But two things of which we can be sure: cages give humans *possession* of the birds inside; and not a single bird is a willful volunteer. Indeed, if *you* could fly free from tree to tree, would you *choose* to spend your life confined inside a *cage*? That choice would even seem absurd to the smallest brain inside the smallest bird.

It is self-evident that *to fly* is the essence of *birdness*. Flying is the characteristic that distinguishes birds from all the other forms of life on this one and only place we know of that has any forms of life. Yes, bats fly. And yes, insects fly, too. Children who paint with their fingers are painters. But *Picasso* was a *painter*. Birds fly, and therefore a bird that is prevented from flying is prevented from expressing the purest form of its existence – in order to salve the whim of someone who is *not* the *bird*.

As flight is to the bird, so *thought* is to the human. It is the ability *to think* that allowed a human to figure out how to capture and cage the bird...and even, like the bird, *to fly*. The accomplishments of the unfettered human mind are astonishing.

But along with the wondrous and *noble* understandings achieved by human minds...are those of the darkest and the basest kind. And these include the

sophisticated cages designed to control – not the
flight of birds – but the *minds* of other *humans*. They
are cages that confine by dictating the boundaries
of what a fellow human *may* think, or *should*
think, and therefore to ensure that all the *other*
things that *might* be thought will *not* be thought.

These cages are systems of belief that enforce
artificial restraints upon the mind. Devious
craftsmen create their cages from materials *within
the minds* of those whom they would imprison.
Unmet needs are a mind cage. *Intimidation* is a
mind cage. *Ignorance* is a mind cage. And fear...
oh, *fear* is a mind cage of the most sinister kind.

The human mind is as evolved to *think* and to
figure things out, as the bird's wings are evolved *to
fly*. *Reason* is the lift that gives flight to the mind
in its quest to understand the *truth* of *what is*.

Belief systems aim to *end* that quest by asserting that
this is what is and ever shall be, world without end, amen.
Yes, you may think *this*. But *no*, you may *not* think *that*.
And to think otherwise is to risk a harm – sometimes
a literal harm, but often the mere *notion* of a harm is

all that is needed; a *vivid fiction* compellingly projected into an unthinking mind. But note that caged *humans* are *willingly complicit in their own imprisonment.*

For there could be no cage without the suspension of disbelief, *volunteered,* by those who are caged. And any thought that does not fit within the confines of the cage is a *threat* to the cage; it is an open door, and a sign that says, 'Go soar!'

A bird possessed inside a cage is something; not a bird. And a mind possessed inside a cage is a burden to behold. We must therefore commit ourselves to lives lived *outside* the cages of belief, within which others would gladly keep us locked for their amusement.

Arise on the winds of thought, I beseech you -- arise!

Insignificant Others

The powers that be
don't care about me;
nor do they care about thee.

Someone Else's Words

When you open up your mouth,
do someone else's words come out?
Then never mind – don't waste my time.
I'll save my ears for the puppeteer,
and skip the puppet show.

It's really such a drag, you know?
To listen as you masticate that moldy leftover
from someone else's kitchen,
inside your wooden mouth.
Something you heard yesterday –
or years ago, on someone else's TV show.
Or a musty mush passed down
from puppets long gone by.
All of which you manage further to corrupt and mutate,
or simply to perpetuate.

The wisdom you received is meaningless to me.
Don't bother making sounds in my direction;
save your putrid puffings for, perhaps, a fellow puppet.

I have a mind that matters – at least it does to *me*.

Ideology is the mummified remains of an idea whose time is *past*.

The Infection Does Not Serve the Host

THERE'S NOTHING ABOUT A CRIPPLING DISEASE like polio that supports the forward progress of human evolution. But let us not forget that humans were nothing more than a medium on which the *polio myelitis* virus fulfilled *its* evolutionary destiny. In its wake were innocent people who could not walk or breathe on their own.

In a similar way, it seems that the effects of *mental* illness are so harmful that they would have been 'selected' out of the gene pool tens of thousands of years ago – if they were transmitted only through genetic inheritance. But what if mental illness is, in whole or in part, the result of a virus acquired from an *external* source, in the same way a flu virus is?

This would account for behaviors that, like the effects of polio, disable its victims' capacities to support their own survival. Compare the behavior of a schizophrenic who hears voices that aren't real, but which may convince him to kill innocent people – or even himself – to the behavior of a rodent infected with the *toxoplasma gondii* (toxo) parasite. This toxo parasite will cause a mouse to lose its primal fear of *cats*, which makes

it easier for the cat to *kill* the mouse, which makes
it easier for the parasite inside the mouse to infect
the *cat*, which was the parasite's intention all along.

The ebola virus survives in the sperm cells of males,
and can infect others as long as a year after a male
victim is *cured*. Polio, toxo, ebola, and countless
other viruses conscript third-party hosts to fulfill
goals that may threaten the lives of their hosts. Why
couldn't a virus that causes physical or mental
illness be clever enough, even, to ride a genetic
relay from generation to generation? We rely on
science to fill in the map of this uncharted realm.

In the meantime, understanding that viruses may cause
self-destructive behavior helps us understand why

victims of *belief* might act in self-destructive ways.

As of this writing, for example, the Catholic Church (one of the longest-sustained belief systems in human history) adamantly opposes all forms of birth control. The *given* reason is that all human life is sacred, and therefore, that to impose artificial interventions on human reproduction is to undermine the will of God. This idea has been systematically reinforced by the Church; so well, that large numbers of children have been a characteristic of Catholic families.

Overpopulation, which can be found within less-developed, less-educated, strongly-Catholic societies, is now a threat to human survival. But viewed from the perspective of the Catholic belief system, overpopulation is an overwhelming *success*. Each generation of believers, unlimited by birth control, is *larger* than the one before. By design, the scale and influence of the Catholic Church thereby expands with every baby born – without regard for the cumulative, catastrophic effect on the host itself. That is, on the habitat we call *Earth*.

As with all viruses, the end purpose of a belief system is the survival of the belief system itself, and *not* the host that it infects.

Beware the Bug that Bites the Mind

Beware the bug that bites the mind –
the bug that reason cannot find.
The bug that makes two of a kind,
then three, and four, and more are blind.

Its victims are the last to know;
their plague transmits on arrowed bow.
And even when the symptoms show,
they proudly watch their fever grow.

Darkness descends with heavy rain.
The uninfected dare not complain;
bug-bitten souls hold *them* to blame.
Lest, God forbid, someone *explain*.

Yet truth and reason vaccinate,
and if embraced, they resonate.
They liberate, inoculate,
against a dull and stupid fate.

And so, dear friend, may I remind –
beware the bug that bites the mind!
The bug that makes two people blind,
and then, perchance, all of mankind.

Human Malware

A BELIEF SYSTEM IS A PROGRAM, installed in a person's mind by someone else, *to serve the interests* of that *someone else*. It will be *sold* as a benefit to the person who is 'programmed'; that is, to the *believer*. But the actual benefits flow in one direction only – to the programmer, as long as the program runs in the believer's mind.

Gentile Germans of the Third Reich were programmed so successfully to believe that Jews were the source of their distress that fellow humans were murdered by the millions. The Nazi Party acquired unlimited power, in part in response to the enemy it *manufactured*.

That is not all it manufactured. It manufactured *monsters* as well, to serve its soulless needs. That's *another* thing that belief systems do. Only the uniforms change.

But belief must be unquestioned and absolute! Because the merest *drop* of doubt is a leak that weakens the dam that holds all the truth out, and all the fantasies, fallacies,  delusions and lies *in*. So thinking must never begin. That's where the *program* comes in. No *thinking* to bore you; it's all been done for you.

Your mind is the membership fee to a group – that's agreed to believe in the same set of fantasies, fallacies, delusions, and lies. From which you may never diverge!

If you should doubt that single condition, then question the tenants of your religion, political party, or other belief system, to others within your group of believers. Note carefully whether their behavior toward you changes in any way – even so subtle as the angle of the eyes or the warmth of a touch. The rule of all belief systems is that you are *all in*, or you are *all out*. Without a *doubt*.

Perhaps doubt was *Herr* Hitler's final sensation before he blew his brains out in the bunker, as truth closed in from all directions.

Prix Fixe

A
belief
system
is like
a restaurant
that only serves
one dish,
and
once you
order it,
you can
never
eat
anything
different
a
g
a
i
n
.

The Ideological Purity Test

This Ideological Purity Test
assures that your thinking aligns
with the thinking that we have decided is best
for us to allow in our minds.

Our Ideological Purity Test
is a test you can never stop taking.
It ensures that you're always as pure the rest;
that you *truly believe*, and aren't faking.

On our Ideological Purity Test,
only one score is ever accepted.
To answer the questions like *we* do is best;
if you miss even one, you're rejected.

We cannot permit any doubt to infect,
for conformity is not a game.
The Ideological Purity Test
guarantees we're exactly the same!

He who spareth the rod
hateth his God.
Thou shalt beat Him
with the rod,
and deliver His soul
from hell.

Lest Constipation Be Celebrated As a Virtue

MIGHT WE ALL AT LEAST AGREE THAT THE SUN revolves around the Earth? Because if the Sun does *not* revolve around the Earth, then why does the Sun arrive every morning in the east, and depart every evening in the west?

Third stone from the sun: Copernicus maps the firmament.

We can therefore agree on this basic
fact, can we not? *Did* we not?

Yes, we did at one time. We *humans*, that is. We
accepted this 'fact' about the world. It made sense
at first glance, so it seldom provoked a *second* glance.
And it gathered a critical mass of presumption. All
those people just can't be wrong, can they?

Well they could, and they *were*. And they were all
proven wrong by a few individuals who *did* take
a second look. As early as 270 BCE, Aristarchus
of Samos thought that Earth might be one of
the spherical planets that circled the Sun.

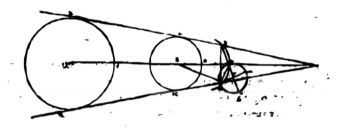

Before darkness ruled the world,
Aristarchus of Samos saw the light.

But his ideas faded away, and 17 *centuries* passed
before Copernicus revived them, in a book
called *De revolutionibus orbium coelestium* (On
the Revolutions of the Heavenly Spheres).
Then Galileo made himself a telescope and
literally took a closer look. Instead of glancing
at the heavenly spheres and then moving on, he
began to *observe* what they looked like, magnified
through his telescope, and how they *behaved.*

By thinking about what he observed, he began to believe that Copernicus' ideas made sense. Galileo wrote books of his own, to document his analysis.

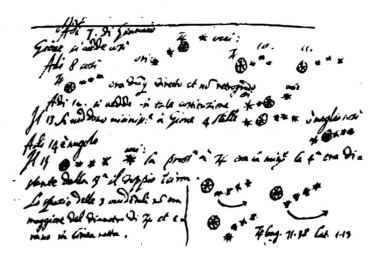

Unfortunately for Galileo, his conclusions were not *politically* correct. It seems they undermined Earth-centric assertions on which the Roman Catholic belief system was built. And since Roman Catholic authority was widely accepted as the proxy authority of God Himself, any idea that subverted the church, subverted *God*. And a *demonstrably correct* idea that conflicted with Catholic doctrine, was the most subversive idea of all.

Galileo's ideas were so subversive that the Church imprisoned him for the rest of his life. *Might* conquered *right*. At least for a while. But right remains right, and as we now know, *reality always wins*. And after fact upon fact upon fact revealed the obstinate error of the Roman Catholic belief system, the Church finally conceded that in fact, those beliefs were *wrong*.

Galileo's insights and observations, which included humanity's first view of the movement of spots across the Sun, required three hundred years *less* time than it took the Church to admit its mistake.

But the message here is more profound than Galileo's unjust imprisonment. The message is also that *each of us* possesses the intellectual capacity to increase knowledge and understanding, and thereby to make things *better*, based on a simple process: *observe, understand,* and *improve.*

For example, you notice a pain in your right wrist one day. You don't know why your right wrist hurts, but your left wrist *doesn't* hurt. Then you notice that the pain manifests itself while you're 'making movies on location' – that is, while you masturbate.

As an experiment, you try switching hands. At first, you find it's more difficult. But with practice, you improve. Meanwhile, with rest, your right wrist feels better. In time, you can use your right hand again. But you have made things better by observing, understanding, and improving an unpleasant reality.

And you did it yourself, with the cognitive power at your fingertips. Maybe it's not as profound as unlocking the behaviors of celestial bodies. But it helped you unlock the salve your *Earthly* body so urgently needed – with either hand! – and *that* might be all the 'profound' you needed just then.

But beware! Beliefs kill cognitive powers faster than

kryptonite! For example, at one time, left-handedness
was taboo. Why? Maybe for no better reason than *it
always had been*. Or because it's just easier to pick on the
few. It's a good thing that didn't stop Leonardo da Vinci,
Michelangelo, Babe Ruth, Mark Twain, Paul McCartney,
Jimi Hendrix, Aryton Senna, or Martina Navratilova.

And the Biblical position on *masturbation?* Why,
agin' it, of course, as illustrated by the story of
Onan, who for legitimate reasons 'spilled (his
seed) on the ground.... And the thing which he did
displeased the LORD: wherefore He slew (Onan)'.

So if you intend to stay cool with *Abraham*'s
rules, self-pleasure is banned, no matter
which hand. As are the cognitive abilities by
which you can personally *figure things out.*

Meanwhile, those who *believe* should thank God
that Onan's sin wasn't voiding his bowels...
lest *constipation* be celebrated as a virtue.

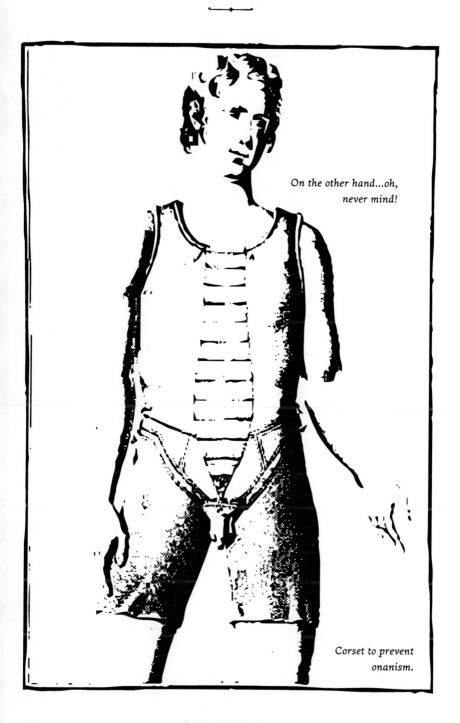

On the other hand...oh, never mind!

Corset to prevent onanism.

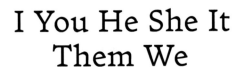

I You He She It Them We

A
Nazi
is a Jew
is a Republican
is al Qaeda
is an Evangelical
is a Fascist
is a Communist
is a Christian
is a Muslim
is a Socialist
is a Pundit
is a Preacher
is an Imam
is a Rabbi
is a Pope.

Make Mine a Single

The single standard's
not the trouble;
my nose tells me
it is the *double*.

Quicker than the Dead

WENT TO A FUNERAL ONCE, OF A MAN I'd known all my life. I travelled 500 miles to join his family and his friends – each to pay our respect for the countless personal moments in which the man had earned it.

We shared a common connection to this man who was no longer present among us, and who never would be again. The funeral, in a small church on the edge of a field, was an opportunity for us to reconcile ourselves with his absence.

He had lived a long, full life, but that knowledge provides limited comfort to those who are left behind. We encountered each other with warm glances and embraces, and with the simple fact of our mutual presence on this occasion.

It was a fine tribute to the man. Memories were shared.
A son spoke with humor and warmth of the father he
had clashed with, and then grown to admire. With
each small story, the bounty of a life was harvested
for a meal prepared by the absent guest of honor.

What more can anyone truly leave behind? What greater
estate may one accumulate than a life well-shared with
those close by? No possession or coin means more than
the moments made better for others. With these, he had
nourished our souls, that we might feed others as well.

And then came the young pastor's turn, to conclude
the formalities. He wore his inexperience as plainly
as his unfamiliarity with the deceased, but he had
a job to do. His job, it seemed, was to conjure a
new story, of an after-life just begun – a story not
based on the actions of the man who died, but
on the presumed needs of those still living.

In this after-life, the pastor said, the man still lived,
though not with us. Now he walked with Jesus through
the pastures of eternity, and I could picture it. The
weather was mild, the soil was soft, the fields were
green, and ever they all would be, as the two strolled

side-by-side. As long as he believed, and we believed, so it all would be. And if that was the price of such a pretty picture, it seemed small enough, indeed.

It's easy to imagine the comfort this final vision brought to the widow and the sons and daughters. But it jarred me from my memory of the man I knew, as if someone had altered his body in the casket to make him look like half his age, or twice his height, or like his mother, or a movie star.

The pastor, as he seemed to feel obliged, invented a story to comfort the survivors, because the life just ended was not adequate unto itself. That life, it seemed, was not enough for the man or for us. So the pastor filled in an imaginary template of a life *still* lived. Not one that we could smell, or taste, or see, or hear, but a common fantasy he expected us to share.

You could see the jitters on the pastor's face, like a young magician hoping he could sell his sleight of hand. But this audience had no interest in engaging disbelief. No matter the ham-fisted execution, the words had been spoken. The tangible accomplishments of the life just ended could now be replaced by a tale of a new life that never ends, which came with no collateral, but the promise that we could share it too, if we just believed we could.

Harold Hill himself could not have said it better. But sufficient unto me is the man I knew in *this* life.

Is Your God?

Is your God the silent type?
Who never says a thing,
but speaks through other people,
or so, at least, they say?
Whose hearsay observations
you are expected to embrace
without a doubt?
Even if the things that you are told
would make you laugh and
shake your head and walk away
if they were the words
of the person speaking,
and not the second-hand,
so-called words of God?

Is your God the psychopathic type,
who lies to keep you ignorant,
or who orders you to kill your son
and then says, 'Never mind.'?
Or has His way with someone else's *fiancé*
when she isn't even *conscious*,
so she can bear a son that He can kill,
so that newborn babies will not
burn in the Hell that He created,
and then sentenced every newborn baby to?
Is that the type of God you worship?

Or does your God provide you *comfort*
as you make your way through life?
Like a teacher who understands precisely

all those things you need to know,
so the bliss of understanding may embrace you?
Is your God as clear and present to you,
always, as the sunlight in the daytime
and the darkness of the night?
Neither obscure nor theoretical,
but as tangible as a dog whose
presence and commitment are unmistakable?
Whose humility is matched by loyalty?

Is your God the reliable type?
The kind who's always present,
sans ambiguity?
Who gives you reasons for that which is,
as well as that which isn't?
Who gives you comfort, not in theory,
not in your imagination,
but directly, like a mother?
With a love that is
unquestionable and unconditional?
The kind that puts an arm around you
in your lonesome moments of fear and doubt,
and holds you close like a father you look up to?
(Not like a father who would kill you.)
Does your God awaken your heart
and warm it every moment,
like the lover who inspires all the best in you?
Like the son or daughter whose life
means more to you than yours?

The Serpent and the Deadbeat

That guy who handled snakes?
The guy who died
when the rattlesnake he handled
bit the hand that handled it?
I wonder what God would say,
if God had not gone so absolutely mute,
so long, long, long ago.

The rattlesnake has raised some doubt
about the words in *Mark: 16*.
It seems to me the words therein
don't mean quite what they seem.
I myself would expect to die,
if I decide to drink a deadly thing.
But if I somehow didn't die,
then I'd think I did not
drink a deadly drink.

The guy who died,
committed to the contract
he perceived in *Mark: 16*.
I admire his commitment
to *his* side of the deal.
He bet his life,
and lost the bet.
But it seems the Other Party
is in breach of the agreement,
which *He* extended, voluntarily.

And once again,
the serpent takes the fall
for a rubber check it
did not write.
And the Silent One
who wrote the check
is never blamed at all.

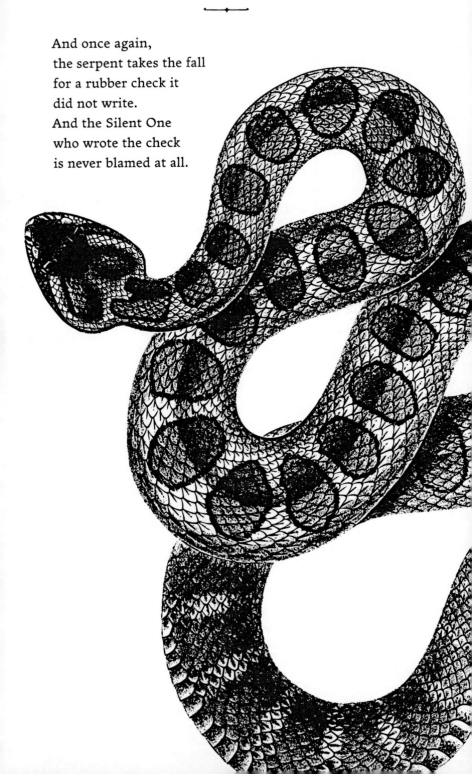

Dominutive

Before we discuss your
'dominion' over every living thing
that moveth upon the Earth,
first, stop breathing for an hour.
Then I will be eager
to hear your thoughts!

Someone Else

Someone else can save the world,
save the world, save the world.
Someone else can save the world;
I've got problems of my own.

Someone else can give a damn,
give a damn, give a damn.
Someone else can give a damn;
I guess I just don't care.

Someone else can figure out,
figure out, figure out.
Someone else can figure out;
I don't know what to think.

Someone else can light the fire,
light the fire, light the fire.

Someone else can light the fire,
and then I will be warm.

Someone else can rescue me,
rescue me, rescue me.
Someone else can rescue me,
and then I will be saved.

Will someone else, please rescue me,
rescue me, rescue me?
Will someone else please rescue me?
I think I'm dying here.

Someone else can die for me,
die for me, die for me.
Someone else can die for me;
I can't be bothered now.

It's all in God's hands... I'm not lifting a finger!

How Carl Became Queen of Norway

OU CAN BE TALLER IF YOU WANT! Actually taller, in your bare feet! I know how you can live in a different time, or live forever – in this material world! You can be thinner, shorter, better-looking, richer than you are – anything you want. Interested? It's easy. All you need is *faith*.

That is, faith that what I tell you is true. If you believe me absolutely, then I guarantee that you will realize all your dreams. I *guarantee* it. Stuck in your failing, 55-year-old body? Want to be a 19-year-old Olympic champion next year? Boom – done! Congratulations, world-class athlete! I said you could do it, and you will. No question about it.

Unless you *fail to believe* that I have the power to make you into anything you want to be, or give you anything you want to have. *That* I can't guarantee. That part of the deal is completely up to you. And I have faith in *you*. But if you have any doubt about me, or don't believe strongly enough in my promise, then I won't be able to make you 35 years younger and more athletically-gifted than anyone else on planet Earth.

That's still a very fair and simple deal: You want something; I do something. You do something; you get exactly what you want. Maybe with a world record thrown in. Sure, why not? You'll set a world record as you win an Olympic gold medal. Next year. Even though the next Olympics are three years away. I can fix that, too.

Not that you're locked into the 'Olympic champion' dream. Remember, I said *anything*. Did you want to be the most beautiful woman in the world? Even though you're a disfigured man? How quickly do you want to catch the eye of every last horn dog you pass by? Tomorrow? Two hundred years ago? Name it, believe me without question or doubt, and it will be *yours*.

How did you think the woman who is now the most beautiful woman in the world *became* the most beautiful woman in the world? That's right – she came to me, and believed without any question or doubt, and I made it happen. Until then, she was a balding, 38-year-old bachelor named Carl with a hairy back, who lived in his mother's basement and kept his toe jam in a jar on the bathroom sink.

But Carl had a dream. A big, sexy, beautiful dream. And guess what? This won't be announced to the public for another month or so...but Carl (now known as Brigitta), has just accepted a proposal from the King of Norway. In a year from now, what once was a homely schmuck without a future will be queen of the most progressive, financially-stable country in Europe. With a baby on the way.

I'm not bragging about this. It was Carl's dream.
Sure, I made it happen, but only because Carl
believed without any doubt that I could. Good
things happen to those who believe in me.

There are, of course, countless others whose dreams
I could have fulfilled. But they just didn't believe
strongly enough. That's the one thing I *can't*
do. Faith is the price of anything you want in the
world. Faith in me. The kingdom of heaven here on
Earth is nigh. Trust me. That's all you have to do.

What Sayest Thou?

I PRAYED AGAIN FOR RAIN today, but today it did not rain again. This must mean I did not pray the proper way, or that I have offended God above, or that this drought is a lesson or a message from my God to me.

Perhaps I should close my eyes tighter when I pray. How else can God the omniscient and omnipotent know the sincerity of my plea? I shall close my eyes much tighter on the morrow. If it rains, I will know that I have provided God with what He needs from me – eyelids clenched tighter when I pray.

If it does not rain tomorrow, then I will know that God has something else in mind. Perhaps my sins too dearly offend Lord God.

Forgive me, I beseech Thee! For I believe in Thy only begotten son, whom Thou hast 'given', so that I might have everlasting life. Please, hear my plea, dear Lord! For I worry less about everlasting life, and more about the next few days, which, without water, will surely cause the death of my beloved children, ages 1, and 3, and 5 – and of my livestock and my crops, upon which my livelihood depends.

Life is my sin. But my faith in Thee is absolute. Is that not Thy expectation? Is there more that Thou require? Is *that* the lesson that this drought would teach me? That more suffering is required? My prayers, my faith, and my suffering – that is, my *continued* suffering – are all I have to give. Except of course, my livelihood and the precious lives of my three children.

Is that the price that I must pay? For which I am left with...nothing? Would that please Thee? Would Thou not at least spare my *children* further agony, and accept *me* as Thy fee, instead? I am not much, but I give Thee all that I have. What sayest Thou?

That our reward is in the next life? But is it not cruel to make them suffer now so needlessly? They are but children. Have they so offended Thee? How, pray tell? And if so, have they not already paid Thee manyfold in distress, at such tender ages?

What sayest Thou, Lord God? You speak a silent language for which I have not ears to hear. But I wish, more than I wish for rain, that I could hear Thee now. That I might understand Thy unmet requirements, that I might humbly fulfill them.

What sayest Thou, if ever Thou sayest, indeed?

Fuckin' the Dog

I asked old crazy Abraham what
he was doin' with that poor
dog. He drove a nail into his
head, and this is what he said:

'I fuck the dog because I know
no better way to demonstrate
my abiding faith in my Lord
Father up above. Except by
killing my son, of course.

'Unfortunately, the Good
Lord has not yet blessed
me with a son to kill.
Instead, He has blessed
me with abundant dogs. And
to honor Him, in everlasting
covenant, I will faithfully
fuck every dog to which
my loins enable me.

'Gee, that schnauzer
sure has fetching eyes!
Praise the Lord, and pass
the lubrication!'

God is Not

God is not the boogie man.
God is not an ass hole.
God does not hold grudges.
God does not play favorites.
God does not play games.
God is not a Republican.
God is not a Christian.
God is not a man.
God is not an American.
Earth is not God's only planet.

Would You Kill Your Child?

Would you kill your child if I told you to? Would you kill your child if someone *else* told you to? Would you kill your child for a million dollars? Would you kill your child for a hundred dollars? Would you kill your child to save your own life? Would you kill your child to save your soul? Would you kill your child if you heard an invisible person tell you to?

Would you consider it morally acceptable for yourself or someone else to kill a son or daughter?

If you would consider it morally acceptable to kill a son or daughter, is there anything you would *not* consider morally acceptable? *Anything?*

What would you think of someone whose life was guided by respect for the killing of a child?

On the Edge of a Prepuce

Is there any truth to the ancient proverb that 'He who hesitates is lost'? It all depends on your point of view, according to a highly-anticipated study released today by the National Association of People Who Think It Would Be A Good Idea To Cut Off Part Of Your Penis (NAPWTIWBAGITCOPOYP).

The study confirmed that eight days is the maximum length of time in which it is safe to circumcise a newborn baby boy. Tests revealed that even one minute beyond the eighth day, when anyone with a sharpened object moved within one meter of their tiny prides-and-joys, every single baby boy involved in the study beat the holy fuck out of the individual with the sharpened object, before harm could occur.

Speaking through several missing teeth, a mohel who participated in the study said, 'The window izh schmall, and it clozhezh quickly. I schould have done thisch yeschterday!'

Baby Jesus casts a wary stare at the last few seconds of his foreskin.

'Terrified to have
any sort of fear.'

'GOD HEAL ME. GOD HEAL ME. GOD HEAL
ME.' So prayed the woman with cancer who
believed, as her televangelist had told her, that
God would heal her, and that to accept the
interventions of modern medicine would be to
choose fear instead of faith in her Lord & Savior.

Then she died.

Did she die because, at the last desperate moment
of her life, her faith had wavered? If so, what
grim judgement would that render on the
Omnipotent One, who could respond with fatal
indifference to the anxieties of a dying woman
who had committed her life to serving Him?

And what would it say about Him if her faith did
not waver, and yet still she died? What reason might
one then give for her death? That everyone dies?
That 'it was just her time'? If so, on what basis was
she allowed to believe He would *heal* her? And why
would it be her time if, without cancer, she would
have reason to expect at least 20 more years of a life?

Why, in fact, would a woman of faith contract cancer?
If good health is not a reward for faith, what is? If
assurance against a premature death is not a reward
of faith, what is? If there is *no* reward in this life for
faith, what then is the purpose? To be rewarded in the
next life, which exists only on the vapors of one's *faith*?

Or were illness and death intended as a *lesson*? If so,
what lesson that might encourage further faith? Is the

message too complicated for a thoughtful
person to comprehend? If so, why?

How could the Omnipotent One have
difficulty communicating such a profoundly
important message, with every power at His
command? Or is the confusion *deliberate*?
Is that part of the divine strategy? If so,
to what purpose? Is the televangelist an
incapable messenger? Why then was he
chosen? Why then does his ministry thrive?

Above all, why the *silence*? Why the mute
response to the misplaced prayers and the
misplaced faith of a desperate woman?
Does it please You to ignore such humble
devotion? When, at any time, You
could clear your throat and
explain Yourself so that *all*
could understand? When You
could raise your hand and
erase the misery of Your most
heartfelt supplicants? Are You
unwilling? Are You *unable*?

If You are unwilling, then I
think You are *cruel*. If You are
unable, then I think you are not
divine. If you are either, then
I think you are undeserving
of my positive regard. Or
anyone else's. I think you
are *imagined*, to meet an

unmet need. I think you are *invented* by the fearful, by
the ignorant, by the desperate, and by the malevolent.

I think that your so-called *divinity* is a vessel
into which much has been poured, and
from which *nothing* can be sipped.

I think the vessel is a fiction. The divinity of life and of
love, and the soul of a dying, desperate woman, are not.

The Last Roundup

EXT. CAMPSITE ON THE CHISHOLM TRAIL – NIGHT

Our bone-tired cowboys sit staring at the campfire, as Slim blows a mournful tune on mouth harp. Ten more days till they get the herd to Abeline. They sure could use some help.

> SOURDOUGH
> Wonder whatever happened to
> *Jee*-sus?

> HANK
> (after a pause)
> Y'know, Jesus was a good one.
> We all miss him around here a lot.
> But he's been gone a long time now.
> I don't think he's comin' back.

Jimmy takes the piece of straw from his teeth and flicks it into the fire.

Charlie farts beans.

FADE TO BLACK

ROLL CREDITS

> Cast of Characters:

Hank..John Wayne
Sourdough...Walter Brennan
Jimmy...Montgomery Clift
Charlie...Walter Huston
Slim...Ben Johnson

What the *Hell*?

I'm confused by that which you expect –
that I might offer you respect,
and wish you and your brethren well...
while *me*, you'd casually condemn to Hell.

Scrutable

'All I can say is that my trust remains
in the Lord,' said the convicted fraud
on his way out of the courthouse.

When asked for comment, the
Lord remained silent.

Engendered

Does masculine mean ignorant?
Does feminine mean weak?
Only to the weak and the ignorant.

You Don't

You don't look like me;
that makes me better than you.
How come you don't look like me?

You don't eat the same food that I do;
that makes me better than you.
How come you don't eat the same food that I do?

You don't diddle the way I diddle;
that makes me better than you.
How come you don't diddle the way I diddle?

You don't believe the same fairy tales that I do;
that makes me better than you.
How come you don't believe the
same fairy tales that I do?

You don't think like I do;
that makes me better than you.
How come you don't think like I do?

You don't live the way I do;
that makes me better than you.
How come you don't live the way I do?

You aren't me;
that makes me better than you.
What the bloody hell is wrong with you?

Make the Boogie Word Go Away!

ARE YOU A'SCARED OF THE BOOGIE WORD? Well, you'd better be, 'cause the boogie word'll *gitcha*. And you don't wanna get got by the boogie word, do you?

So, if I say, **'TERRORIST!'**, you do anything I say to make me *not* say **'TERRORIST!'** again. Got it? If I say, 'Invade a country that is not a threat, or I'll say **"TERRORIST!"** again', you say, 'Yes, sir! Invade away!'

If I say, 'Abandon all your legal, moral, and ethical principles, or I'll say **"TERRORIST!"** again', you say, 'Consider them abandoned! Starting now!'

If I say, 'Bankrupt your country, destroy your economy, and hand the debt to your children and your grandchildren, or I'll say **"TERRORIST!"** again', you say, 'To hell with my children and grandchildren!'

Because boogie words are *sca*-wee! They make you want to suck your thumb. You might even need to poop your pants. Make the boogie words go away! Boogie words are the most terrifying things you can imagine!

And there are lots of boogie words:

SOCIALIST!

SECULAR!

BLASPHEMY!

SINNER! INFIDEL!

LIBERAL!

HUMANIST!

ATHEIST!

APOSTATE!

SCIENCE!

HERESY!

PROGRESS!

TERRORIST!

RADICAL!

TERRORIST!

TERRORIST!

And these are just a few! So, when you hear a boogie word, don't forget to be scared. After all, they're *scary*!

But don't worry! If someone says a boogie word, all you have to do is anything the person who says the boogie word *tells* you to do. *Anything.* That's how you make a boogie word go away!

Then you can stop sucking your thumb. And *then* you can stop pooping your pants.

'I don't like confrontations,' said the doormat to the jackboot.

The Last Nickel

FLIM AND FLAM wanted all the money. They didn't *need* any more money than they already had. They had more than ever they could spend, or their children's grandchildren or *their* great-grandchildren could spend. They wanted more because they *decided* they wanted more. Money did not make them better people, or nicer, or more talented, or more useful, or more attractive.

Wait – it did make them more attractive. At least to people like them, who measured beauty not by the vastness of one's soul, but by the vastness of one's assets. For no one can deny that money can buy things, and more money can buy more things. And things bring comfort to some. Not things that one needs to survive – like food, or shelter, or good health, or love.

For Flim and Flam and those attracted to their money were not in need of the necessities of life. Their comfort could be assumed. No, the attraction lay in the potential to obtain *unnecessary* things. Necessary, that is, only to amuse for a moment those bored with their existing collections of unnecessary things. And whose status among their peers could only be sustained by the escalation of possession.

So that one might say in a casual way to a rival on a Saturday, 'I bought a new *thing* today.' And then lean back and allow the envy to circulate. Followed quickly, in the minds of the envious, by the contemplated possession of the new thing in question, with a flicker of admiration at the notion that this thing was the perfect thing to buy. 'Why didn't I think to buy it?' Then a sadness in the aftertaste. Then the seeds of a plan to identify an even *better* thing to buy, to even up the score. *Things* are a form of currency for those who have too much, and those who have too much cannot relax until they have a little more.

Flim and Flam wanted more...and more, and more, and more, and more, until one day there *was* no more. After close accounting, Flim and Flam had gathered all the money in the world. Exactly half by Flim, and half by Flam. *Minus* five remaining cents. Dear God, a nickel still existed somewhere in the world!

Not a trivial amount at all, for Flim or for Flam. Not another thing, in fact, possessed any value at all except this last remaining nickel, to either one of them. Oh, never would their stomachs growl, and never would their shoulders shiver from a lack of warmth on the coldest winter day. Every comfort would always be assured. Every ailment quickly cured.

And yet, distress consumed the two. In someone's pocket, somewhere, rested that last and final nickel. In someone's pocket, but not in either one of theirs. It was, therefore, the only thing that finally mattered. But who would find it first?

No expense was spared, as you could surely guess. No piggy bank was too obscure. Somewhere, somewhere, somewhere, somewhere, that precious nickel would appear, to end the game in Flim's favor, or in Flam's. No palace could exceed the value of this final coin. Eternal life itself could not compete. All consequence and value drained from all things everywhere, and all that mattered to the only two that mattered was a single, simple nickel, and the possession thereunto.

Elsewhere, unaware, inside a Kmart vestibule, you could see young Hector standing there, studying his options. Hand inside his pocket, with the store about to close. Not simply to close for the day, you understand, but to close *forevermore*. No one had any money left – that's just the way it was. What need for stores, except those few that Flim or Flam still owned and patronized? But this store was not one of those – just a shell of empty shelves. Useless by tomorrow, then awaiting excavation in some unfathomable future, like the frame of a once-but-now-no-longer-deadly *siats meekororum.*

Hector had discovered that his options were reduced to *one*, having surveyed the other empty gum ball machines. He turned the nickel over in his pocket. It was a precious nickel, you see, because it was the last of Hector's summer lawn-mowing money, which he would therefore spend most carefully.

But now, having saved it so long, there remained but one gum ball machine in which to use the nickel, with only two gum balls left inside. One yellow and one red, and thus the crux of Hector's nickel. Red – *cherry* – the best of all gum balls in the world! And yellow – *lemon* – the worst! Sweet or sour – which one would it be?

He turned the nickel one last time, withdrew it from his pocket. He drrropped the coin right into the slot. He twisted the handle, and the noisy gears inside seemed amplified as they gave his humble hopes a ride.

He opened the flap...and out rolled the cherry
red gumball! How complete the world could
be! Oh, nothing could exceed the joy of that
first sweet bite of cherry gumball!

And then the store was locked with
chains, and forgotten to this day.

And Flim and Flam lived out their lives, miserable
and shattered, in the hopeless quest to find the
final nickel. They found no comfort in all the
other things around them, for only could that
five-cent coin bring value to their lives.

How You Gonna Pay For Your Dandy Little War?

A PERSON WHO TAKES WAR LIGHTLY is a fool. So never let anyone convince you to participate in, or in any way to support, an unnecessary war.

How can you tell if a war is necessary? It's easy.

If every political leader who enables the war is required to serve the highest-risk roles in the highest-risk locations, *without exception*... then it just might be a necessary war.

If service in the highest-risk roles and locations is also based on family income (the higher the family income, the higher-risk the assignment), *without exception*...then it just might be a necessary war.

If every citizen between the ages of 15 and 40 is required to serve in combat roles, *without exception*...then it just might be a necessary war.

If every adult citizen is taxed at 25% of gross income to finance the war itself and the medical care of the survivors (in addition to all other taxes) until the last survivor no longer needs it, *without*

exception...then it just might be a necessary war.

If, and *only* if, not some, but *all* of these conditions are met, continuously, *without exception*, over time, no other way out, you've wracked your brain, you're at a loss, unfortunately, sadly, regrettably, un*thinkably* – then you may *begin* to con*sid*er the possi*bil*ity that you may per*haps* be dealing with what some *might* describe, *under certain circumstances*, as that horrific thing that some luckless victim of said circumstances (though I hope to Christ almighty that it is not you, or me, or anyone we ever knew, or anyone whoever was or will be born) *might* be forced to call, for want, dear God, of a better word...a necessary fucking war.

Under no other circumstances should you support the war in question. See? Simple.

Unless you are a fool. But you're *not* a fool.

Are you?

Dumb Guys With Guns

Bury the bodies
and bang the drums...
deliver us all from the
dumb guys with guns!

I implore, by the light
of 10,000 Suns!
Deliver us all from the
dumb guys with guns!

Lest right maketh might,
then the end has begun.
Deliver us all from the
dumb guys with guns!

Deliver us all
from the dumb guys
with guns!

Pocket Bomb

There's a bomb inside my pocket...
I put it there myself.
It tells me when I'm A-OK,
and when I do not feel so well.

This bomb inside my pocket,
it goes off all day long.
I'm pleased when it agrees with me.
It interrupts me when I'm wrong.

It nags me and it tags me,
it hears everything I say.
It shares my conversations
with strangers far away.

It tells me where I am right now,
and where I'm going to.
It's not surprised when I arrive
by bus in Katmandu.

The bomb inside my pocket,
the one that I put there,
takes pictures of me anytime,
and posts them *everywhere*.

It plays me songs, it reads me books,
it is my telephone.
It comforts me with certainty
that I never am alone.

My pocket bomb delineates
my identity.
It assures me I am special,
that I am worthy of its fee.

If my friend should find a better bomb,
my pocket bomb finds out,
and leads me to a *better* bomb,
so I never have a doubt.

I love my bomb,
my bomb loves me.
If I should ever lose my bomb,
then I would cease to be.

The Alchemist's Apprentice

A TALENTED YOUNG CHEMIST WAS DETERMINED to make her mark. Her professional success would earn her personal wealth and happiness. All she needed was a significant accomplishment.

Along the way, she had befriended an elderly man who studied the lost art of alchemy. In the waning days of his life, he discovered the secret that had eluded alchemists for centuries. He had figured out how to turn worthless lead into priceless gold!

Knowing that his life was almost over, he invited the young chemist to his lab to reveal to her his undocumented secrets.

As he began to talk, she felt the device inside her pocket buzz. Who could it be? It was a message from a friend, who wanted to make plans for the evening. Without the alchemist noticing, she quietly began exchanging messages with her friend. Should they go see a movie? Where would they eat?

They figured out a plan. It sounded like fun. In fact, it would be the perfect way to celebrate this most important day of the young chemist's life. She signed off. She slipped the device back into her pocket and resumed listening to the alchemist, prepared to capture all his detailed notes.

At that moment, he looked at her with the most glistering smile she had ever seen. 'And *that*,' he said, 'is the secret!'

And all she heard were those last five words.

'Wait – *what*?'

And then the alchemist died.

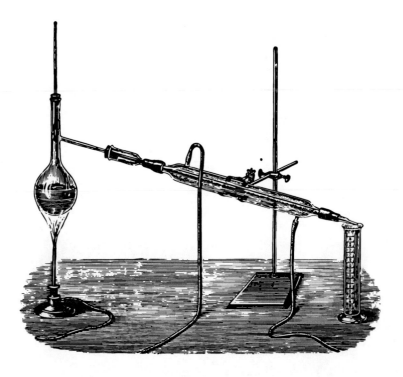

Always and Forever

I just heard about this new technology! It's new! It's revolutionary! It's going to change everything! It's...already obsolete.

I just heard about this new technology! It's new! It's revolutionary! It's...already obsolete.

I just heard about this new technology! It's new! It's... already obsolete.

I just heard about this new technology! It's...already obsolete.

I just...wait...I am still here. Neither obsolete, nor with the intention to be.

And though I often benefit from the technologies
that come and go, technologies are not me.
Nor would I ever want them to be. They do
not make me more myself. They do not make
me wiser, nor better than someone else.

Oh, they bring me ease, and help protect me from
disease, and serve as tools to do the task at hand more
handily. I would not wish the *absence* of technology,
which is the offspring of our unique capacities.

But technology must suffice to be my servant, not
my master. When it no longer serves my dignity,
then technology is no friend to me. A useful
tool, indeed, but only when it serves *my* need.

I will not allow technology to obliterate my humanity.

Cool, as in Cadaverous

'I pierced my eyelid yesterday,
got seven new tattoos.
I'm running out of things to do
with all this oxygen I use.'

Having all become so cool,
may we now aspire higher?
So much cool becomes the drool
that extinguishes the fire.

I yearn for more integrity,
and less that is so hip.
Sincere is revolutionary,
a noble flame to light this trip.

Oh, call it cool and hawk it,
if profit makes you dance.
As long as courtesy's the product,
we all might stand a chance.

Monkey *mee*, ...

Whatever you say is what I want to say.
Whatever you see is what I want to see.
Whatever you do is what I want to do.
Whatever you are is what I want to be.

Second verse, same as the first...

Fools Believe

Fools believe if they believe the world is flat,
then the world indeed is flat.
They believe the strength of their belief
is a virtue to behold.
But the world remains round.
And they remain fools.
Without virtue.
To behold.

Unlocked

Do you feel safe inside that box,
protected from the world by locks?
Do you think that I should live there, too –
locked in darkness next to you?

Should he and she and *tout le monde*
squeeze inside your tombish home,
so we can safely wait to die...
and then ascend into the sky?

There are no walls, and I am free
of locks that only you can see!
I'll leave you to fellate your thumb;
I have undiscovered chords to strum.

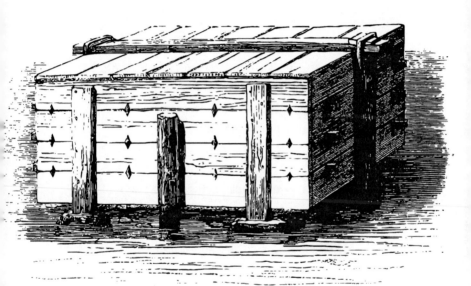

As I Die Living

Alarm went off. Got up. Microwaved a frozen sausage biscuit. Opened up a Diet Coke. Finished breakfast. Shit. Saw blood. Took a shower. Got dressed. Drove to church. Heard some words. Prayed. Shook some hands. Drove home. Got cut off on the highway. Didn't honk. Parked in the garage. Sprayed some weeds in the driveway. Went in the house. Put on replica of my favorite player's jersey. Turned on the football game. Jacked off. Wind blew outside. Leaves fell off my trees. Couldn't see my lawn. Didn't like the leaves on the lawn. Waited till half time. Went out to the garage. Fired up the leaf blower. Put on my ear protection, so I didn't have to hear it. Put on my mask, so I didn't have to smell it. Blew the leaves off the lawn, into the street, so I wouldn't have to pick them up. Lawn looked better. Gassed up the leaf blower. Ready for next time. Went back in the house. Ordered a pizza. Watched the second half. Farted. Watched another game. Fell asleep in my chair. Whatever.

'Maybe I'll die before I have to do this!' said the optimistic procrastinator.

Yesterday's Fire

Yesterday I intended to gather wood for the
fire, but the day was too appealing to waste
in such an effort. Instead, I savored sunshine
and contemplated clouds. When the day was
done, my soul felt soothed. What a pity it would
have been to miss out on such a perfect day.

Today it snowed, and the stove stood colder
than the air around it. I warmed myself
with memories of yesterday's bliss, and
waited eagerly for the next warm day.

The Stick Up My Ass

There's a stick up my ass, so you'll suffer, too! And
you, and you, and you, and *you*. Feel the discomfort
of the stick up my ass. No, *be* the discomfort
of the stick up my ass. Not pleasant, is it? Nor
is it meant to be. Its intention is only to bring
pleasure to *me*. That is, to share, shall we say, the
pain in my ass, so we both may suffer equally.

And you are wise not to ask why -- why the stick up
my ass, and why I keep it there. That is, unless you
wish to compound the pain I inflict upon you, as a
consequence of the self-inserted stick up my ass.

Do you see that my pleasure derives from my misery?
My glorious, magnificent misery! Shared, by intent,
between you and me. What reason would please me
more than to darken the light that might sustain *you*?

Ah, that precious, perpetual stick up my
ass! Long may it trouble your days!

Posteriorism

'Nothing means anything,' said Foucault.
'Yes, it doesn't,' said Derrida;
then each deconstructed up his own ass.

And now,
Foucault is fool's gold,
and Derrida is Derridead.

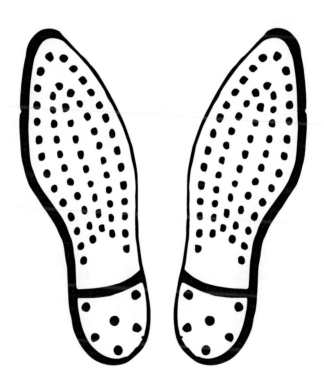

Nothingness

OTHING MATTERS, DOES IT? The future. The planet. Your family. Your life. Who cares? Nothing means anything. We're all going to die, aren't we? No one cares. Why should I care? Why should you care? It wouldn't matter if some stranger walked up and shot you right now, would it? Or shot your dearest loved one to death, right in front of you. Raped your little sister while you watched. Poisoned all the water in your town. Pissed in your coffee or shit in your soup. You don't care. I don't care. Nobody cares.

Nothing exists. This world isn't real. You don't feel cold. You don't feel hot. You don't feel anything, because nothing is nothing is nothing is nothing. Anything you say is true, I say is a lie. Anything you don't say is true, I say is a lie. Hear what I say. Everything is a lie. There is no love. There is no beauty. There is no joy. There is no life.

Death is our salvation! Death! No anything. Eternal darkness. That is all that we desire. The end of all. All is broken, all is finished. All things created are over! Done! Nothingness, nothing, nothing, nothing, nothing. Nothing must be. No light. No light. No light. No life. No hope. The end of all. Chaos. Misery. Destruction. Madness. Fear. Pain, sweet pain. Despair. Agony and death.

Death of all things. Death of sky. Death of water.
Rancid, deadly poison water. Death of fish. Death
of fowl. Death of flowers and death of all trees.
Death of all children. Death of their dreams. Death
of all dignity. Death of all honor. Death of all
truth. Death of all decency. Death of all justice.
Death of all freedom. Death of all wisdom.

Death of the sparrow. Death of the cloud. Death
of the worm. Death of the grass. All life from
microbe to whale, from tropic to glacier, all of it
dead. All of it dead. Rejoice in the death. Rejoice
in the nothing. Rejoice in the rot. Rejoice in
decay. All of it, all of it, all of it gone. And nothing
remains. Limitless nothingness, darkness and void.
Deliver me, dear god, to thy darkness and void.

All of the valiant generations of life, all of them gone.
Every moment to moment duel against death, gone
without trace. Gone without thought. Gone without
care. A newborn fawn on spindly legs. An alpine
blossom shivering in the breeze between two rocks
above timberline. A baby gorging at its mother's breast.
Gone! Gone in the glory of nothing at all. Thy will be
done. Thy end of all things. Nothing meant anything,
and all of it gone. All of it, all of it, all of it gone.

Destruction is the quick work of cowards.

Creation

is a campfire
on the dark side
of the moon.

Make things better!

The Mighty Light of the Candle in the Cave

IGHTNING STRUCK THE DRY NEEDLES ON THE FOREST FLOOR, and a small fire began to burn. An antelope bounded from behind a nearby bush. The curious one observed. Fire destroyed, but fire warmed and illuminated, too. A controlled fire could be useful.

This would require three things, he reasoned: a repeatable means by which to start a fire, a source of fuel, and a means by which to move the flame at will. He began to experiment, mastering one challenge at a time. Lest he be ridiculed by the leader and the others, he worked in private. Or so he thought. But while he worked, his curious children observed. As they watched his work progress, they wondered why he did not share his impressive secrets with the others.

One night, a storm drove the group inside the sacred cave, where all shivered in the darkness. 'Tell us again,' said a woman, 'of the secrets of the sacred cave'.

From where he stood, deeper into the cave than the others in the group, the leader began to speak.

'Behind me lies the dragon that guards the portal to the afterlife. You are safe to touch his slimy fangs, should you feel yourself so brave. But do not step beyond his fangs, for it is his duty to protect the afterlife from this life, and this life from the afterlife.'

As they always did, the group took a step back from the dragon's fangs, toward the entrance of the cave.

'Let us beseech the dragon, who
protects us,' said the leader.

'We thank thee,'
said the group as one,
'for the work that you have done.
We pray we will not anger thee.
And on the day our race is run,
we pray you guide us mercifully,
unto a safe eternity.'

'May we always please him!' murmured members
of the group in comforting refrain.

For a moment, the rain outside made the only sound. No fear or need troubled anyone among them. Until suddenly, a woman spoke. 'Where is my baby? She was beside me, and now she's gone!'

'Reach out around you,' said the leader. 'Our many hands become our eyes in the darkness.'

'We must find her,' cried the woman, 'before she crawls beyond the dragon's fangs!'

'She must be close at hand,' said the leader. But no one spoke up. No one could find the small child in the lightless chamber. The curious one understood the mother's anguish. And he knew his portable flame might provide enough light to find the wandering child. But what would the others think? What would the leader think?

'Please, someone find her!' said the woman. Panic filled the cave.

From a pouch, the curious one removed the flint and the crude candle he had fashioned. He struck a spark, and held forth a tiny flame. The others gasped, as though the curious one cupped the Sun itself within his hand. They backed away, uncertain and confused.

But he moved confidently among them, having practiced with his self-made flame. His children celebrated with a silent glance between them. In the shifting shadows, his daughter quickly scratched a small drawing of an elk on the wall of the cave.

'There's the baby!' said the curious one, several
moments later. 'Beyond the dragon's fangs.'

'Those aren't dragon's fangs,' said someone
near the leader. 'Look – they're only pointed
rocks!' In the candle light, a bead of water
elongated and fell from the point of a stalactite,
to the point of the stalagmite underneath.

The mother grabbed her baby.

'We have angered the dragon!' said the
leader. 'All must leave the cave!'

'But it's still raining!'

'All must leave the cave at once!'

In a reflex response to his authority, the reluctant
group made its way out into the storm. The
leader smiled secretly as the rain extinguished
the fragile candle. Sudden curiosities were
likewise drowned by the cold, persistent rain.

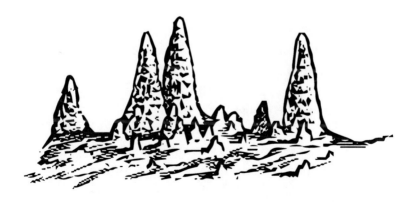

The next day, the rain moved on. The
leader found the curious one alone. 'You
have discovered a new magic,' he said.

'It's not magic at all,' said the curious one. 'I
simply figured out how fire works.'

'Will you join me today on a private hunt,
so that I may better understand?'

A private hunt with the leader was the highest
honor among the group. It would allow the
curious one to better share his discoveries
with the group. He eagerly agreed.

They discussed many things on the hunt that day,
though the nature of the dragon was not among

them. They found themselves not far from the
sacred cave as the Sun began to fade. As the curious
one turned toward the snapping of a twig, the
leader drove a spear between his shoulder blades
so deeply that the handle of the spear broke off.

In the last light of day, the curious one's
children saw the leader drag something into
the cave. They did not follow him further. The
leader dragged the body deep into the darkness
of the chamber, beyond the 'dragon's fangs'.

In the following days, the leader told the group of
how he and the curious one had become separated
on the private hunt. He had searched for the curious
one until the light was gone, but was not able to find
him. Perhaps he had fallen off a ledge. Or so angered
the dragon that the dragon had devoured him.

Those brief, illuminated moments inside the cave were
not spoken of again. The children of the curious one
were wise enough to keep their counsel to themselves.
But having watched their father conquer flame, they
quietly created a new version of the candle. Their
improvements would have pleased their father.

On the night that they had finished, at the
entrance of the cave, unseen by others, they
lit the candle and stepped inside.

Learning to Learn

MAGINE YOU AWOKE ONE DAY on an unfamiliar planet. You had no idea where you were or who you were. You had no memories. You had no idea how to communicate with the beings who surrounded you, but they were large and smart and powerful, unlike you. Your survival would depend on their ability to understand your needs and then respond to them. With no past and no instruction, guided only by their responses, you would have to learn to survive in this unfamiliar place.

Does it sound like an impossible challenge? Like a nightmare? Maybe a lost episode of *The Twilight Zone*? Or a situation only a highly-skilled survivalist could figure a way out of? It sounds that way to *me*.

And yet, one day I found myself in those exact same circumstances. I kid you not!

But guess what? So did *you.*

And so did everyone you ever knew.

Each one of us arrived without a clue, as refugees in an unfamiliar land, on the day that we were born. And all the skills that we acquired since then are the result of our ability to *learn*.

In fact, the saga of our lives is the transition we
each make from a state of knowing *less* to a state
of knowing *more*. We start out knowing nothing;
we are helpless packages of urgent needs. As
we grow, we learn more about ourselves and
the world around us. What do we like? How do
we feel? How do we acquire what we need?
Each insight enhances our ability to engage
successfully with the reality we find around us. On
our own, we learn. Informally, by repetition and
imitation, we learn the nuances of our native language
– vocabulary, grammar, idiomatic complexities.

We learn to *learn.*

And then one day, it breaks my heart to say, some of
us decide we've learned *enough.* And on that day we
die. Our bodies still exist, but not the souls inside.
They are done that day, and we are done that day.

But others of us learn until the day we die,
and thereby *live* until the day we die.

Where They Stopped is Where We Begin

TO PUT AWAY CHILDISH NOTIONS IS NOT to
invalidate childhood. Childhood is a stage – a necessary
stage. But to cling to childhood is to consume the seed
before it has a chance to take root and bear fruit. It
is to undermine the natural rhythm of a life. There
is a time to be a child. Adulthood is not that time.

The myths and stories that reinforce belief systems
are immature indulgences; childish comforts. It
is long past time for us to gain adulthood as a
species, and to leave such childish things behind.
Maturity, in this case, is the price of our survival.

We do not respect our ancestors by fossilizing their
farthest forward progress, or their mistakes, or their
misplaced beliefs, no matter how earnestly they came
to be. We respect them by recognizing that their
understandings were formed by the best information
they had in their time. But each new generation has an
obligation to further the journey, not to celebrate our
ancestors' stopping point as the best we, too, can do.

Where they stopped is where we begin. To remain
where they left us is to fail them, and to dishonor their

progress forward. Our obligation to those past, present, and future, is *embetterment*, as best we can encourage it.

Mariners and Cartographers

I count on you
to tell me what is true.
I do the same for you,
and when we do,
we stand a better chance
of finishing the day
in the most *positive* of ways,
in a safe and joyful place,
among the people whom we love,
who also made *their* way in safety
through the tempests of their day,
by the lines on charts that warned them
where the shipwreck rocks awaited,
hidden by the waters that
appeared to offer safety,
but that in fact disguised
a danger that persisted.

The mariners and cartographers
who *proceeded* us, you see,
left a gift that we may now improve upon
in some new and unknown way,
though we may not chart the sea or rocks,
but may convey an altogether *different* gift
to travelers yet unborn.

Oh, joyous gift of life
that we are privileged to receive!
Let us share our wisdom purposely,

that we may mitigate the suffering
that will sometimes trouble *we*.

Let us not concoct confusion,
but assist in understanding
all the riptides and the reefs
that we ourselves have seen,
so that others make safe passage
by virtue of the knowledge
of those dangers,
which were noted most precisely!

Dead Broke⋆

If something in your life is broke,
you got to fix it now.
You may not have the ways and means,
but you must find a how.

If something in your life is broke,
you must not hesitate.
Delay exacts an interest rate,
you can't afford to wait.

If something in your life is broke,
don't let it gather dust.
Fix it yourself, or get some help,
or you will fall to rust.

⋆ *(the high cost of entropy and apathy)*

What's An Honest Person Left to Do?

RE YOU SURE? That thing that someone told you – are you sure? Are you sure that he or she or they or it knew any more than *you*, of which they spoke? Did you question the veracity of the assertion? Or the motive of the speaker? What evidence did he or she or they provide? Any evidence at all? Or did you just accept the things they said were true, because they had the nerve to say them, and you assumed that they knew more than you?

If so, why did you assume? Have you no mind to use yourself? Does someone tell you what to eat, and when? Does someone tell you what gives you pleasure and what does not? On whose authority are you so told? On mine? But how on Earth could I know? How could *anyone*, indeed? Anyone, that is, but *you*? So why should I or he or she or they presume to tell you what to feel, or what to think, or what is true? Unless, of course, there's something I or we or they want *out* of you. Some kind of gain that follows from your unquestioned acquiescence.

'Up is down and day is night and 2 + 2 is 5. You understand these things of course, do you not? I would not wish to share your shame in believing these things somehow not so! How dreadful would that be? How unfortunate for you! But I can see that you can see that 1 + 1 is always 3...obviously! So we agree. And now you sign this line, and what is yours will now be mine, because you can clearly see that 1 and 1 is simply 3!

'Congratulations on our new relationship! For your convenience, I'll deduct your payments automatically on the 1st and 15th day of every month. In return for which you'll be relieved of the disgrace of misunderstanding anything I might have said that results from inadequate capacity in your ability to recognize that up is down and day is night and 1 + 1 is 3. D'accord? Mais oui! Obviously'!

So by virtue of your standing there, someone else said something, and in your civility you accepted what was said, because you assume a *reciprocity* in sincerity and veracity...is that the way it happens? A courtesy extended? Oh, it should not be a source of doubt – at least it should not *have* to be.

For without such presumptions of good intent, there could be no society. Without such presumptions of good intent, we would devolve back to that state of nature from whence we once arose. Suspicion and hostility would poison every moment. 'Kill or be a morsel' would be our eternal, exhausting pre-occupation. Not the easiest way for *homo sapiens* to make their way from B to A. Better for a lion or shark or *tyrannosaurus*, shall we say?

And yet, and yet, and yet, and yet. Preditation lurks among those who walk upright on two legs. Though they might not *seem* a threat, or appear to be a danger, they lurk here and there, and maybe in your underwear. They may preditate with malevolence, they may preditate with greed, they may preditate with ignorance, but they preditate to meet *their* need. Not *your* need. *Their* need. And *you* may be their need.

They will make it easy as they can for you to meet their need. No money down, and they will leave you be. For now. You mean well, and because you have a soul that feels, it is not your nature to resist the ostensible need of a fellow passenger who captures your attention. If you are able to assist in reducing the discomfort in this passing moment, it would not occur to you to *not*. You would trust that someone else would do the same for you.

In fact, your kindness rests on this good faith. It is the epoxy of society. And it is the faith on which malevolence most often preys. *I would not take advantage of* you, *therefore you would not take advantage of* me. More often than not, he or she or they or it might *not*. Then again, they *might*. Maybe one in every ten, or one in every twenty. No matter, they are there, and you'd be well advised to be aware.

It's not as hard as it might sound. Just don't *forget* to be aware. Perhaps the last ten people you entrusted proved worthy of your trust. Perhaps the next ten will, as well. But eventually, as the Sun is hot, I promise you that one will *not*.

So what's an honest person left to do? One who would do unto others as you would have them do unto you? Simply this – *do not assume*. Instead, *insist*. With all the courtesy that fits. Demand a reason. Check the math. Use your gut if gut you must, but examine all the evidence, and *then* bestow your trust. Or *not*, if the numbers don't add up. Then add them up again, and ever after. *Always question each assumption*, even those you've certified were true.

Is it true today? Is it true right now? Why? How?

How about *now*?

They Taught Themselves to Fly

All creatures that fly have wings.
Humans do not have wings.
Therefore, humans cannot fly.

It's plain to see that God did not intend the human race to fly. As it was and ever shall be. *Oui?*

That's a point of view that would have been easy to support...until the 17th of December, in 1903. At a place called Kitty Hawk, a mile or two from the Atlantic, in North Carolina, USA.

On that day, the idea that humans could not fly became *obsolete*. All of human experience was written new – by a pair of bicycle mechanics from Dayton, Ohio, who had not a single day of higher education between them. Let us pause to ponder these facts.

Neither Wilbur nor Orville Wright was born with wings. Nor were they born into a family of wealth, and the advantages *that* brings. It may have been possible for them to continue their education beyond high school, as their sister Katharine did, but neither Wilbur nor Orville so chose to do.

Instead, for reasons only they could say, they chose to apply themselves to the previously-unconquered challenge of human flight. Again, let us ponder. If the challenge was to be met, it would not, directly at least, be met with the only other means by which the challenge had ever been met before. Because humans are not equipped with wings.

But they *are* equipped with *minds*. Wilbur and Orville Wright had minds. I have a mind. You have a mind. And what are human minds designed to do? Above all, they are designed to *figure things out*. To solve problems. To modify or better understand what *is*, and to make it something better.

The knowledge of Will and Orville – the Wright brothers invent aeronautics at Kitty Hawk, 1901.

Lots of sentient beings are capable of modifying their
environment to improve their lot. Birds make nests.
Beavers build dams. Spiders spin webs. But within the
natural realm of figuring things out, humans have no
rivals. Like it or not, for better or worse, humans have

so conquered the planet that our only true predator is
humanity itself. (And we are a lethal predator, indeed!)

But the Wright brothers had *other* concerns in mind.
They contemplated the challenge of artificially-
propelled human flight, and they concluded that,
unlike every other human who had walked the Earth
before them, *they* could meet the challenge. 'For
some years,' wrote Wilbur, 'I have been afflicted
by the belief that flight is possible to man.'

And then they *did* so, with neither public nor
private financial support. Without computers,
or advanced degrees. Without, in fact, much
support of any kind, save that of Charlie
Taylor, a mechanic in their bike shop.

But they would rely profoundly on their *minds*, and
on a process common to all those who figure things
out. It is a simple process that can be summed us as
'Observe, Understand, and Improve', or OUI. Those
familiar with *la langue française* will recognize '*oui*' as
the French word for 'yes'. Pronounced, it sounds like
the English word, 'we', which means 'me and thee'.

By applying the principles of OUI to their chosen
challenge, that is, by observing, understanding,
and improving each element of the problem they
encountered, two unsung individuals, far from the
celebrated platforms of prestige, accomplished the
previously impossible. *They taught themselves to fly.*

Whether the Weather

NTENNAE UP!
Yep, you've got sensors. Everybody does. In fact, *every living thing* does. Our sensors keep us alive. They bring us information about the world around us. That's important, because everything changes all the time. Everything. All the time.

Without antennae to tell us what's different and what's new, living things like me and you don't know how to respond to these changes. We don't know how to *adapt*. To adapt is to surf on the waves of life. To recognize the *beat*, and to join in the song.

Everything is beatin'. When you syncopate with every beat, you no longer simply live – you then become *alive*. But if you do not hear the beat, or you think you can *reject* the beat, oh, here comes *trouble* down the street.

Hear this. A cat doesn't notice that the weather's untethered. Doesn't pay attention. Antennae down. Other things distract his mind. And he does not care that much for *coats*. But the weather don't care whether he cares, or whether he does not.

Which he discovers, in spite of his inclinations, late one autumn evening, when he dips out the door in a t-shirt...and into a blizzard. Now, his *skin* gets the scoop right away. But the news to his brain is *waylaid*. So he goes on his way, convincing himself that the bebop is cool, though the bebop is actually *cold*.

He misses the beat. Slow on the uptake. Up on the downbeat. Attempting a song that is rhythmically wrong. No signal, all noise. His radar is jammed; he's unable to jam. Jammed by *himself*, for reasons not clear to those in the groove.

He catches a cold. He curses his fate. But who is to blame? *He* is to blame. For ignoring the rhythms he was born to improvizate. Listen, my dude, I implore unto you...diggeth the beat, and the beat will dig *you*.

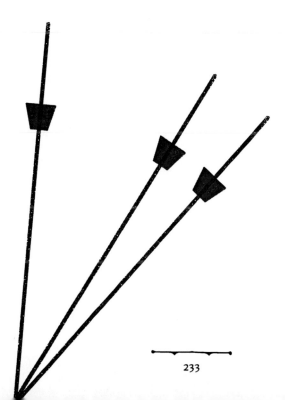

Emotion Does Not Contemplate

Let us accept that we are human, and emotion is the engine that drives us onward through the blizzards and the blazes of our lives. We love, we hate, we fear, we envy, we desire, and we deceive – sometimes all at once.

What are we to do? As humans, we are inhabited by emotions. Without them, we would not be human. But they often propel us sans direction or control. 'I want' is not a patient or a careful impulse. Lovers crossed. Possessions purloined. Lives ended. Sorrow sewn.

'I want' in its primal form does not consider
what consequence might lurk between desire
and result. It tracks down a fix, then looks
for the next. And the next. And the next.

Emotion serves many purposes. Civilization is not
one of them. One may question whether civilization
is a worthy achievement. And yet as a species,
humans seem compelled to gather and to civilize.

But not through emotion alone. For all of its
raw appeal, emotion does not contemplate,
reason, or plan. It does not experiment or
understand. It does not improve itself.

And yet *we humans do*. Because the engines of emotion
we are born with *do* come with controls that, if
mastered, allow us to *harness* our emotions, and to

guide them toward destinations of the nobler kind.

These controls, which exist in our *minds*, are often neglected; neither understood nor valued. To be sure, they are not as easy to activate as emotions are themselves. But though it might seem a long way from amygdala to the prefrontal cortex, it's all right there, right now, inside that crazy thing that's balanced on the top of your neck, and mine. Both the emotions, and the mind that can find the more admirable path.

Desire is universal in the animal realm. An emotion can plant the urge to perpetuate the species, or to visit some curiosity at the farthest edge of eyesight. But our *minds* allow us to unlock the principles of aeronautics, design an aeroplane, build it, and fly it there. And then, to keep on going.

Life is sometimes a process
of revisiting the same lesson
until it finally is learned.

Change Abides

Change abides
in tempests' tides,
and kittens' pads
on the garden path.

Honor the Connections

Disconnection is an illusion.
Every bug, bird, tree, and sea
is part of you and part of me.
No matter our philosophy.

'I am he as you are he
as you are me and
we are all together.'

The plant casts a seed,
the bird eats the seed,
the man eats the bird,
the worm eats the man,
the worm turns the soil,
the soil gives birth to the plant,
the plant casts a seed.

I fear only fear
and the confusion that it breeds.
From confusion comes
a needless kind of harm,
and fear does not protect me.

But as I honor the connections,
I am here, and I am well.

Sittin' on Top of the World

 MOONDOGGIE IS A COOL, COOL CAT. He paddles out to find the biggest wave, and when it comes, he knows *exactly* what to do. He times the break just right, and when the moment comes, he pops up on his board and *skills* his way into the curl, to that perfect spot where the water does the work and his feet have all the fun.

Check him out! Standing on a piece of wood, with his arms spread out like wings, and grins to light his way. This ain't just a second-hand wall of water assaulting the sand upon some beach – it is an engine of delight, a partner in Moondoggie's pleasure.

Damn! He finishes one wave and paddles back out to catch another. The next one, he knows, will be a wave like the one before, but *not exactly*. Faster, slower, taller,

sooner, bigger or not, but *never the same wave twice.*
This is why Moondoggie always paddles back out again.

If you'd never even *seen* an ocean, you would
appreciate his skills. Oh, he can make it look easy,
but you know it isn't easy. But somehow out there
in the surf somewhere, Moondoggie acquired
the understanding of the balance and the wave
dynamics that it takes to ride the surf. A lot of tries,
and most likely a lot of failures, but each time he
understood the requirements a little bit better.

Then one day, *he could do it.* So that's good, and
that's impressive, but that's not what draws him
back out to the ocean, day after day after day.

It's the *difference from one wave to the next* that
stirs old Moondoggie's soul, and demands the
moment to moment adjustments he may never
have made before, and may never need to make
again. But *this* moment requires *this* adjustment,
and *that* moment requires *that.* The pleasure is
what comes from adapting to each challenge *as it
happens,* and finishing off the wave successfully.

What he cannot do is surf each different wave is if
they were the same. He could try, but he would fall.
What fun is falling? What does falling demonstrate? It
takes no skill to fall. Instead of an exuberant glide up
to a bikini-filled beach, ending in a jaunty dismount,
a wipeout is a way to see what sand feels like against
your face, when your face is underneath a ton or
two of water. And all your friends are watching.

Moondoggie weighed his choices: learn the ways of the wave, and adapt as they come, or be pummeled by insisting that the waves accommodate *him*.

Or he *might* have weighed those choices, if he wasn't Moondoggie. But the joy is in the *surfing*. Every cool cat knows that!

Unless you like
the taste of sand,
learn to surf
the changes, man!

Plum Tree's Request

The leaves on the tree are winking at me;
they want me to say something nice.
I scratched my chin and began to begin,
by agreeing to take their advice.

Some people need people, some people are strange,
some people are as dumb as a turd.
Some people are proud of refusing to change,
and some people, they don't mean a word.

But beige or black or purple or pink;
if the roof is on fire, if the rainwaters rise,
someone will appear, and hand you a drink –
someone with compassionate eyes.

Walls disappear with emergency near.
Sans political parties, religious beliefs,
or deceptive invocations of fear
(which corrupt a pure gift of relief).

I will always insist better angels exist
under blankets of darkness and greed.
Let us thrive, not merely subsist!
(With which all of the leaves have agreed.)

Persistence

The delicate roots
of a tiny flower
cling hopefully
to the grains of soil
collected from the winds
in the crack of a cold chunk of granite
on the shadeless side of timberline.
Moment by moment,
it gathers photons
from the Sun
and fulfills
its bold task
with the grace
of the divine.
It *lives!*

Each Seed Invests Its Hope in You

Does it matter if you live or die?
And do you have a reason why?
Do you need a reason to survive?
Or have circumstances stolen
all the light before your eyes?
And all the hope within your heart –
has it gone missing, too?

I understand that empty feeling
of hopelessness and helplessness,
and the damage it can do.
It's not a decent thing
for good people to go through.

But in spite of what the dogmas say,
and how you did or did not start this day,
you can find a place to play,
to sing the things you have to say,
to create a more delightful day,
upon the beatin' path.

Comfort and encourage each
precious seed of selflessness and truth.
Transmit the joy each rooted seed then brings.
Then comfort and encourage
yet another tender seed,
and another, and another, and another –
caring not how small the seed may be.
For each seed invests its hope in you.

Hoping you will open all the wonder
that awaits within the seed,
and therefore within you.

How Long?

How long since the last time you asked 'Why?'
How long since the last time you figured something out?
How long since the last time you used solitude
as a time to think, without distractions?
How long since the last time you did
something you've never done before?
How long since the last time you read for pleasure?
How long since the last time you laughed?
How long since the last time you did something
kind for another living thing, without the
expectation of recognition or reward?
How long since the last time you left
something better than you found it?
How long since the last time you reconsidered
something you were taught or told?
How long since the last time you ignored a fear?
How long since the last time you refused
to let someone else define you?
How long since the last time you
learned something new?
Not long ago at all, I hope!

The Universe
Within

Pay no mind
to the skin, so thin;
invest your time
in the universe within.

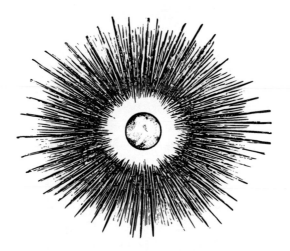

Always At Your Fingertips

VERY DAY, PEOPLE STOP ME ON THE STREET and say, 'I don't know what to do! I don't know what to do!'

I just smile and say, 'Listen to this, my friend.' And then I tell them:

It may not seem this way, but there is a system you can use to *think* your way through almost any situation. It's worked for me. It can work for you, too. But put your money away. I'm not here to sell you anything. This is not a financial transaction, though some people might prefer it if it were.

Some might wish that a simple transfer of cash would at the same time relieve them of the responsibility for the action that's at hand. 'I pay the way – you save the day.' But that is not the way this works.

No, this way, you save your *own* day. You are the hero of this and every other tale you might apply it to. It turns out you already have that secret superpower you have always wanted.

Wait...did you just hear what you *think* you just heard?

Indeed you did, and there's an easy way to find it.
Make a 'number one' with your left index finger.
Touch the tip of that finger on your left temple. It's
on the side of your head, right around the corner
from your eye. Leave your left finger there.

Now, make a 'number one' with your right
index finger. Touch the tip of that finger on
your right temple. Leave it there, too.

Close your eyes. Direct your awareness to
the area between your fingertips. Take all
the time you like. This is important.

Because in fact you have just located the most unique
place in the universe; the divine spring from whence
your most precious capabilities flow. That's right – you
already possess that superpower you always wished
you had. It's the mind that comes from the prefrontal
cortex that waits *right now* between your fingertips.

With it, your fellow humans have figured out the
evolutionary process of life, split the atom, learned
to fly, visited the moon, composed symphonies,
bounced messages off satellites in real time around
the world, developed vaccines against horrid
diseases, painted masterpieces, built cities, and
developed universal principles of human rights.

These accomplishments may seem beyond the
reach of you, me, and our fellow mundane mortals.

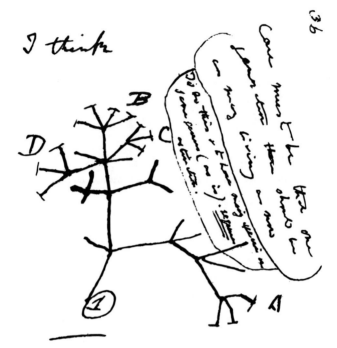

Charles Darwin did some thinking...and figured out
how life interacts with time. Voilà – evolution!

But the celebrated people responsible for those achievements were mundane mortals, too. Mundane mortals who learned how to use their superpower minds to *figure things out*. And you can, too.

I'm not saying you'll discover a medical breakthrough, though you might. And I'm not saying you'll write the most beautiful song ever sung, or find the lost city of Atlantis. Though you might.

What I am saying is that you have a gift. You have, *within you*, *right now*, a tool with which to accomplish more than you can imagine. You have a paintbrush, a canvas, and a box of paints, my friend, with which to leave the world better than you found it, 'whether by an improved poppy, a perfect poem, or a rescued soul'.

Your mind is your art, and we can't wait to see your masterpiece. But the tool lies dormant and useless, until you choose to use it. It is not mine to use, or anyone else's. Only *yours*.

And it's always at your fingertips.

You Can Think!

RE YOU TIRED OF TWITCHING like a splinter-headed puppet, every time some swindler slides a dishonest word out the side of his or her manipulative mouth?

Are you ready to immunize yourself against the virus of belief that has infected humanity since the world's first liar crossed paths with the world's first fool?

Do you want to chop the chains and seize the reins of the forces of fulfillment that await you, less than an arm's length away from wherever you are right now?

It won't cost a fortune. It won't cost a *thing*. Critical thinking will activate that sleeping superpower between your left ear and your right ear, and launch you on the great adventure you were *born* to take!

Before you know it, you'll be:

- Questioning assumptions
- Challenging authority
- Reasoning
- Figuring things out
- Making things better
- Fulfilling your divine potential

Sound hard? It's not.
You can think in bed.
Think on a couch.
Think in a car.
Think in a bar.
Think in the bath.
Think on a path.
Think by the sea.
Think when you're three.
Think when you're laughing, or shopping, or cooking,
or sleeping, or working, or staring at the sky.
You can think when you're rested, or
tired, or eating some pie.
You can think when you're thinking about nothing at all.
Think when you're playing with a kitten or ball.
Thinking is food for your mind, that's all!

So why not start thinking for yourself, right now?

Together Through Time

On the beatin' path, we grow, and live, and discover. We live life from the inside out. We are more today than we were yesterday, and we will be still more, tomorrow. We are ourselves, unique, and at the same time we are a part of all things.

Practice finds the beatin' path. Practice seeking truth where it may lead us, every second of every minute, with hearts full of wonder, joy, good will, and compassion for the struggle of all creatures great and small, and all of the living things that accompany us on our journey together through time.

We are watchful and wary, always, of the doctrines that infect the minds of good people, and lead them into darkness.

Instead, openness and reason light our path, that we may earn true passage on this eternal trip.

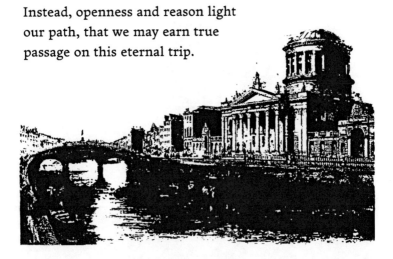

Conquer Your Impatience

Did you speak your native language
on the day that you were born,
understanding all the nouns and verbs?
Or did it take some time for you to master
all those unfamiliar words?

And the first time you controlled a bike,
was it the first time that you tried?
Or did you try, and fail, and try again,
until you learned the skills to ride?

It takes a little practice to communicate and go;
a little effort every day.
Let *practice* conquer your impatience,
and you'll be on your way!

This Instrument of Life

Oh, I love to watch a baseball game.
I love to hear the Beatles sing.
I love to see a well-made movie.
How less my life would be without them all,
and the immeasurable bliss they bring.

But I am not the second-hand experiences
that sometimes occupy my time.
To live, to me, is to live first person –
tasting with my own tongue,
loving with my own heart,
thinking with the mind of
no one else but mine.

I live to make things better,
for me and *tout le monde*.
But borrowed joys are not enough.
So I practice every day to improve this
instrument of life I play,
rejoicing in the song released
within my DNA.

A Test of Skills

Every moment
of every life's
an experiment;
every moment is a
test of skills:

In this
one and only
holy moment,
how well will I adjust
to this
one and only
holy curve ball
that life is
throwing at me
now?

John 'Doc' Lavan awaits the pitch.

Two Blue

Someone said,
'The sky is red.
As any fool can see.'
I swallowed my uncertainty,
since I did not wish a fool to be.
I seemed to earn his company
as soon as I agreed.

Someone else said,
'One plus one is three,
upon which sum I earned my Ph.D.'
Having bypassed higher education,
I nodded at her explanation.
Silence thus preserved my reputation.

My friends and fortune multiplied,
and all I had to do was hide
that silly little itch inside.
It seemed a simple price to pay
to keep the loneliness away;
a meager fee to subsidize
my popularity – that is,
with everyone but *me*.

'How like the sky,' I said one day,
as I watched a blue jay fly away.
And then another, which made *two*.
'But no one else must hear me say
these blasphemies I observe today!'

For Hell awaits, if not on death,
then in *this* life,
bereft of the approval of
those who insist only that
that which I can plainly see,
must instead be something that
separates reality from me.

And yet it was not Hell that
overwhelmed me, but a
weightlessness of soul,
as if I sat upon the blue jay,
camouflaged against a sky that
is not blue because I tell it to,
or you, or you, or you, insist it not.

And Hell is but a rot I rent
to curry someone's company,
until I understand that neither
he nor she nor it nor they
ennoble me.
Then I appreciate *my* company.

And as long as fortune blesses me with a
companion committed to the true,
then lift your eyes and you will see us
soar inside a sky so
elegantly blue!

We are here and it is now. Amen.

The Holy Whole

If genuflect
you feel you must,
then kneel no less
to the whole of life
than you would
to the sacred cow.

If There Be God

I study the eloquence of the poppy in bloom and think surely, if there be God, *here* be God. There must be some practical purpose for the sublime aesthetic of flower and pod – to attract the bee, perhaps. If so, the bee is clearly pleased. What a glorious pair they make, the poppy and the bee!

I have no further need for evidence of some divine intention. Life itself is sufficiently humbling, magnificent, unfathomable. These collections of energies and designs, organized from the most random and indifferent of raw materials, united in a single purpose – *to continue* – they are the manifestation of whatever the sacred spirit may be. Life is God, and God is life. No more, no less. No doctrine, no time. Locked boxes of beliefs, myths, traditions – all fail in the face of the unfiltered forces of life.

My religion is the Sun-tippled leaves of a cottonwood tree, the voice of a bird, a seed – all seeds – and the fertile homes they seek to find. Every living thing is a miracle unto itself. We may discover the genetic and molecular materials from which life arranges itself, but we must bow our heads at the patience and persistence with which these raw materials have configured themselves to find new ways to

adapt to the circumstances which confront them,
and thereby to continue – individual to individual,
generation to generation, day after day, each fulfilling
its role in the passage of its kind through time.

Life is the perpetuation of complex collections of
energies – a system that wrestles order from the
inevitable adversities of entropy and time. It is a work-
around, a compromise, a miracle, if miracles there
be. What an honor it is to be *of* it and *among* it for this
stage of the never-ending relay through time. Nature,
civilization, the manifestations of life – *this* is my
church. No more, no less. If there be God, *here* be God!

If You Believe in Cleveland

If you believe in Cleveland,
then buddy, you believe in dreams.
The past is vast, the present tense,
the future isn't always what it seems.

If you believe in Cleveland, Steven,
then you believe in truth.
In every sullen sunset, even
you will find the proof.

If you believe in Cleveland, honey,
then you believe in me.
I am here and you are there,
but we will always be.

The Yins and the Yangs

Life, alas, is not a straight line.
But isn't it fine that it's not?
The plot gets thick in the zigs and the zags,
 on the way to the *denouement*.

What happens next,
I can't wait to find out!
Will today be the day
when the big ship comes in,
or a more typical day on the way?

The longer I wander
the yins and the yangs,
the more I'm intrigued by it all.
Do the wise have a chance?
Will the fools win again?
Will the robins and roses
return in the spring?
And what will this Saturday bring?

Light the Light

Pay attention, raise a doubt,
be the one to figure out.
Apply yourself, surprise yourself,
do not rely on someone else.

Light the light upon the land;
make your mind, and make a plan.
Deliver unto all the true –
the universe expects you to!

Wonder Awaits

The beatin' path
is the golden path
that may never have been
travelled before.

The first prints on the path
may be *yours*, my friend,
or you may find it well-worn
since before you were born.

Oh, the beatin' path
is not the *beaten* path;
a fool will never find it.

But wherever you are,
it awaits your next step –
if it's light that you seek,
good will fills your heart,
and truth is the North Star
that guides you.

Walk on, now,
walk on, now,
walk on...
wonder awaits!

Manifesto

Hey there – flower on the tree!
You and me together, let us
manifest our destiny.
And that is only just
to be, to be, to be, to be...

The Beatin' Path

I raise a glass
and I tip my hat
to Arthur J Stanley, Jr
my Grandfather

With love and thanks to all who have helped and inspired me along the way, including (in approximate order of appearance):

Carolyn Lane, Adam Lane, Ruth Stanley, Richard Lane, Elizabeth Lane Crain, Elaine Stanley, all my aunts, uncles, cousins and their families, with an extra nod to Dr. Bob Andrews, Susan Hoffman, Richard Andrews, Sherman Yunghans, David Yunghans, Zane Yunghans, Johnny Lane, Ella Lane, and Cathy Vader, Dorothy and the Blackwells, Dr. Seuss, Mark Twain, Firecracker, Beulah Walker, Bessie Stanley, Danny Kaye, Hans Christian Andersen, Satchel Paige, Lewis Carroll, John F. Kennedy, the Mercury 7 Astronauts, Don Marquis, Shakespeare, Rod Serling, Jim McKay, The Beatles (the coolest older brothers a guy could ever have), Muhammed Ali, Bert Campaneris, Aesop, Jose Tartabull, Frank and the Matsons, The Beach Boys, Steve Violett, Peebles, Fran and Harvey Oathout, Bonnie and Jack London, Kip Burkman, Lawrence S. Ritter, Bennett Rodick, Irving Baker, Elsie Jett, Chuck Berry, Bob Dylan, O. Henry, Gene Gilmore, Mike Rips, Simon & Garfunkel, Upton Sinclair, Mahatma Gandhi, Clarence Darrow, Jim Fuxa, Rob Crossman, Jim Ryun, Stanley Kubrick, Arthur C. Clarke, Jean-Claude Killy, The Doors, Arthur Penn, Harper Lee, Robert F. Kennedy, Martin Luther King, Jr., Claudia Eilbeck, Mark Ziegenbein, Cab Calloway, Roger Bannister, Frank Shorter, Jack Bachelor, Steve Prefontaine, Paul McCartney, Paul Simon, George Orwell, Stevie Wonder, F. Scott Fitzgerald, Mari Wahl, Luther MacNaughton, Marian Nelson, Dave Sink, Jack Churchill, Rod Patterson, Kim Young (Sky Pilot, come in!), Rick Burger, Dan Almgren, Vincent Van Gogh, Edgar Degas, Pablo Picasso, Bruce Crain, Fred Goss, Edward Dorn, M.C.

Escher, Jack Kerouac, Neal Cassady, David Broderick,
Steve Rizzo, Bruce Springsteen, Tom Waits, Buddha,
Gary Snyder, Steve Beauchamp, Tom Wolfe, Ken Kesey,
Hunter Thompson, Bernie Morson, Marianne Potter,
Andy Maikovich, Sue Digby, Albert Hoffman, Ed White,
Myron Young, James West, Ethel Blackwell, Tom Avery,
Pops, Cornell Clements, The Clash, Marilyn Megenity, Jan
Lierl Merten, Barry Merten, Celia Siebert, William Blake,
Patrick Crowley, Curtis Casewit, Orson Welles, Sergei
Eisenstein, Ron Roybal, Marshal McLuhen, Quentin
Fiore, Jerome Agel, Prince, Lao Tzu, John Lennon, Eric
Hoffer, Al Papst, Ed and Karen Mitsch, Tom Nicholson,
Greg Banse, Buckminster Fuller, Big Joe Turner, Nicola
Tesla, Benoit Mendelbrot, Hank Williams, Brian Vines,
Jim Bonne, Thomas Paine, Kerm and Sondra Peters,
Mehitabel, Forrest Ciesol, Lenny Bruce, Johnny Johnson,
Adam Mealman, Johnny Lane, Benoit Trufanow, Yvonne
Fair Tessler, Maggie Welch, Jon Pinnow, the young man
who stood up to the tanks in Tiananmen Square, Carolyn
Hales, Marc Munden, Judy GeBauer, Gabriella Cavallero,
Gordon Burgett, Erik Sandvold, Jon Wilkerson, Jamie
Horton, Alfred Hidalgo, Nik Mills, Joyce Meskis, Akira
Kurosawa, Toshiro Mifune, Miyamoto Musashi, Max
Watkins, Park Peters, Regina DeLeon, Todd Robertson,
Connor Lane, Bill Mount, Karen Storsteen, Peter Hansen,
Edward de Vere, Pat Kunkel, Steve Nasstrom, Larry
Bograd, Bob Bows, Mark Gipson, Dianna Bull, Steve
Lavezza, Rob Chalecki, Michael Watson, Mo Mahany,
Wilbur and Orville Wright, Norma Mae Isakow, J.M.
Coetzee, George Harrison, Phil Antonelli, Spike Stockdale,
Skip Bell, George Peknik, Madeira Aftab, Charles Darwin,
Alec Rothrock, Robert Zubrin, Thich Nhat Hanh, Tim
Lane, J.K. Rowling, Blip, Abraham Lincoln, Stephen

Colbert, Eric Burden, Gail and the Hartmans, Mira Wiley, Rose Wiley, Caroline Avey, Jose Clausell, Ron Miles, Janet and Carter Burgess, Deshawn Jones, Rumi, Coleman Barks, Charla Bevan-Jones, Micaela Jones, Stella, Mark Bliesener, Steve Kadi, Patty Stillwell, Steven Johnson, Dr. John Snow, Hugh G. Gauch, Jr., Albert Einstein, George Inai, Neil deGrasse Tyson, Steven Johnson, Francis Bacon, Lucretius, Johann Sebastian Bach, Banksy, Christina Lammerman, Gin Pollock, Anile Prakash, Leonard Cohen (there'll be no cooler guy in town, as long as Leonard Cohen is around), Brian Wilson, Martha Wainwright, Richard Heighway, Keith Richards, Shulem Deen, Jason Siebert, Duke Ellington, Wayne Horvitz, Sean Carroll, Joan and Marcus Nashelsky, the Grateful Dead, Robert Hunter, Henry David Thoreau, Dave Ratner, and many more, I hope, to come...

A BEATIN' PATH PLAYLIST

There's a Place (*The Beatles*)
It's Alright Ma (I'm Only Bleeding) (*Bob Dylan*)
Brown-eyed Handsome Man (*Chuck Berry*)
That's Just What You Are (*Aimee Mann*)
The Rising Sun (*George Harrison*)
Ship of Fools (*World Party*)
Good Thing (*Paul Revere & the Raiders*)
Sun is Shining (*The Fireman*)
Reason to Believe (*Bruce Springsteen*)
Big Rock Candy Mountain (*Harry McClintock*)
Johnny Appleseed (*Joe Strummer & the Mescaleros*)
Wonderful World, Beautiful People (*Jimmy Cliff*)
I Know There's an Answer (*The Beach Boys*)
Getting Better (*The Beatles*)
Beautiful (*Carole King; demo*)
Brave New World (*Blue Stingrays*)
Take It As It Comes (*The Doors*)
It Was a Very Good Year (*Frank Sinatra*)
Everybody is a Star (*Sly & the Family Stone*)
Stand! (*Sly & the Family Stone*)
(What's So Funny 'Bout) Peace, Love,
and Understanding? (*Elvis Costello*)
The Happening (*Diana Ross & the Supremes*)

CITATIONS

All best efforts have been made to properly attribute all of the illustrations contained in this book. All are used with permission or in the public domain. Most are more than 100 years old. Artists are noted if available.

- Cover sunflower adapted from Wikimedia Commons: Large Sunflower (Flos Solis Maior), plate 1 from part 5, B. Besler, *Hortus Eystettensis*, 1713 edition.^*
- Solarium shell illustration adapted from *Animals: 1,419 Copyright-Free Illustrations of Mammals, Birds, Fish, Insects, etc. A Pictorial Archive from Nineteenth-Century Sources.* 1979, Dover Publications, Inc.
- The British Library collection, from *The Tiber and the Thames: Their Associations, Past and Present.* 1876.**
- Panther adapted from *Animals: 1,419 Copyright-Free Illustrations of Mammals, Birds, Fish, Insects, etc. A Pictorial Archive from Nineteenth-Century Sources.* 1979, Dover Publications, Inc.
- Hiragana by Mira Wiley, 2016.
- Chapter headings adapted from The British Library collection, from *Lyrics of Lincoln's Inn, etc.* 1896.**
- Leroy 'Satchel' Paige of the Negro League Kansas City Monarchs on the mound, UNDATED. Getty Images. (Photo by National Baseball Hall of Fame Library/MLB Photos via Getty Images) Used with permission from Getty Images.
- Satchel Paige photo, undated. Used with permission from the National Baseball Hall of Fame Library, Cooperstown, NY.
- Sunflower adapted from Wikimedia Commons: Large Sunflower (Flos Solis Maior), plate 1 from part 5, B. Besler, *Hortus Eystettensis*, 1713 edition.^*
- Sparrows adapted from Wikimedia Commons: Illustration of Abd al-Kuri Sparrows (female above, male below) from *The Natural History of Sokotra and Abd-el-Kuri*, 1903. Engraved by the firm of Bale & Danielsson, Ltd. after an original by Henrik Grönvold (1858–1940), from a contribution by William Robert Ogilvie-Grant (1863–1924) and Henry Ogg Forbes (1851–1932) to a work edited by Forbes.+*
- Bird tracks adapted from Wikimedia Commons: Bird Tracks, uploaded by Magnus Manske, 2011. Creative Commons (https://creativecommons.org/licenses/by/2.0/deed.en)
- Portrait adapted from The British Library collection: *The naval and military history of the wars of England, including, the wars of Scotland*

and *Ireland, etc,* 1800.**

- Map adapted from Wikimedia Commons: *The shape of Earth,* as envisioned by Samuel Rowbotham, 1881.^*
- Athletics, Oxfordshire, England, 6th May, 1954, Roger Bannister breaks the tape as he crosses the winning line to complete the historic four minute mile record (Photo by Bentley Archive/Popperfoto/Getty Images) Used with permission from Getty Images.
- Cholera map adapted from Wikimedia Commons: Original map made by John Snow in 1854.+
- John Snow photograph adapted from Wikimedia Commons: Autotype 1856, published in 1887. Creative Commons (https://creativecommons.org/licenses/by/4.0/deed.en)
- Quill/paper illustration adapted from 3,800 *Early Advertising Cuts: Deberny Type Foundry,* 1991. Dover Publications, Inc.
- Author's collection: *Sphinx moth lifecycle,* 1857
- Finches adapted from Wikimedia Commons: *Journal of Researches Into the Natural History and Geology of the Countries Visited During the Voyage Round the World of H. M. S. 'Beagle' Under the Command of Captain Fitz Roy,* 1890. Robert Taylor Pritchett (1828-1927) Based on a photograph from the Freshwater and Marine Image Bank at the University of Washington. Materials in the Freshwater and Marine Image Bank are in the public domain.
- Cactus adapted from the British Library collection: *Das republikanische Brasilien in Vergangenheit und Gegenwart, etc. [With illustrations and maps.]* 1899.**
- Brain cross-section from Wikimedia Commons: *Die Frau als Hausärztin,* 1911. Mann and Welb. This media file is in the public domain in the United States.*
- Sextant illustration adapted from from Wikimedia Commons: *Nordisk familjebok,* 1904. This image was first published in the 1st (1876–1899), 2nd (1904-1926) or 3rd (1923-1937) edition of Nordisk familjebok. The copyrights for that book have expired and this image is in the public domain, because images had no named authors and the book was published more than 70 years ago.
- Wolf illustration adapted from *Animals: 1,419 Copyright-Free Illustrations of Mammals, Birds, Fish, Insects, etc. A Pictorial Archive from Nineteenth-Century Sources.* 1979, Dover Publications, Inc.
- Whale illustration adapted from the British Library collection: Biodiversity Heritage Library: *Herrn Johann Anderson, I.V.D. und weyland ersten Bürgermeisters der Freyen Kayserlichen Reichsstadt Hamburg, Nachrichten von Island, Grönland und der Strasse Davis, zum*

wahren Nutzen der Wissenschaften und der Handlung, 1746. Creative Commons (https://creativecommons.org/licenses/by/2.0/)
- Cliff swallow adapted from the British Library collection, Biodiversity Heritage Library: *American ornithology; or, The natural history of the birds of the United States v.3*, 1870. Creative Commons (https://creativecommons.org/licenses/by/2.0/)
- Adapted from Flickr photostream/Eric Fischer: *Amoeba, The World Book*, 1920. Creative Commons (https://creativecommons.org/licenses/by/2.0/)
- Pine cone illustration adapted from *Plants: 2,400 Royalty-Free Illustrations of Flowers, Trees, Fruits and Vegetables*, 1988. Dover Publications, Inc.
- Brain illustration adapted from Wikimedia Commons: *Traite complet de l'anatomie, de la physiologie et de la pathologie du systeme nerveux cerebrospinal*, 1844. Creative Commons (https://creativecommons.org/licenses/by/4.0/deed.en)
- Photo of Buzz Aldrin adapted from Wikimedia Commons: by Neil Armstrong, 1969. This file is in the public domain in the United States because it was solely created by NASA. NASA copyright policy states that "NASA material is not protected by copyright unless noted".
- Lascaux cave painting adapted from Wikimedia Commons: Prof saxx, GNU Free Documentation License. Creative Commons (https://creativecommons.org/licenses/by-sa/3.0/deed.en)
- Helios illustration adapted from Wikimedia Commons: *Manual of Mythology, In Relation to Greek Art*, 1890. Unidentified ancient Greek painter. +*
- Galileo illustration adapted from *Fondo Antiguo de la Biblioteca de la Universidad de Sevilla*, 1854. Creative Commons (https://creativecommons.org/licenses/by/2.0/)
- Sun illustration adapted from *3,800 Early Advertising Cuts: Deberny Type Foundry*, 1991. Dover Publications, Inc.
- Shaving brush illustration adapted from Wikimedia Commons: *Agricultural bulletin of the Straits and Federated Malay States*, 1902.**
- Venus flytrap photo adapted from Flickr/Mark Freeth: *Welcome to hell – Mono. Nightmare!*, 2014. Creative Commons (https://creativecommons.org/licenses/by/2.0/)
- Trap illustration adapted from Flickr/Fondo Antiguo de la Biblioteca de la Universidad de Sevilla: *Lello universal em 2 volumes : novo diccionário encyclopédico luso-brasileiro / organizado e publicado pela Livraria Lello sob a direcçao de Joao Grave e Coelho Netto. - Porto : Lello*

- Smiling monster illustration adapted from The British Library collection: *Travels in little-known parts of Asia Minor; with illustrations of biblical literature and researches in archæology. With maps and illustrations*, 1870.**
- Clock illustrations 1, 2, and 3 adapted from Flickr/Compendium of Illustrations/Patrik Tschudin. Creative Commons (https://creativecommons.org/licenses/by/2.0/)
- Playing card illustration adapted from Wikimedia Commons: *Jolly Nero*. This work has been released into the public domain by its author, Trocche100 at Italian Wikipedia. This applies worldwide.
- Night/Day illustration adapted from The British Library collection: *Geography*, 1894.**
- Fool illustration adapted from *3,800 Early Advertising Cuts: Deberny Type Foundry*, 1991. Dover Publications, Inc.
- William F Buckley, Jr photo adapted from Wikimedia Commons: Univ of Michigan, 1970, taken by Arnielee. Creative Commons (http://creativecommons.org/licenses/by-sa/3.0/)
- Cow illustration adapted from The British Library collection: *A Treatise on Milk Cows, etc. [Translated from the French.]* 1847.**
- Inhofe photo adapted from Wikimedia Commons: *Jim Inhofe, Senator from Oklahoma*. This United States Congress image is in the public domain. As a work of the U.S. federal government, the image is in the public domain.
- Frame adapted from The British Library collection: *Försök till beskrifning öfver Sveriges städer i historiskt, topografiskt och statistiskt hänseende, efter de bästa tryckta källor samt med många tillägg*, 1855.**
- Face of the fool illustration adapted from: *The Fables of Aesop*, illustrated by Richard Heighway, c. 1894.+*
- The ass in lion's skin illustration adapted from: *The Fables of Aesop*, illustrated by Richard Heighway, c. 1894.+*
- Hands with coins illustration adapted from: *The Fables of Aesop*, illustrated by Richard Heighway, c. 1894.+*
- Boss illustration adapted from The British Library collection: *La Russie ancienne et moderne, d'après les chroniques nationales, etc*, 1855.**
- Hand illustration adapted from The British Library collection: *Cloister to Altar, or, Woman in love*, 1890.**
- Plant illustration adapted from The British Library collection: *The Muses of Mayfair. Selections from vers de société of the nineteenth century. Translations from the French and German*, 1874.**
- Palm trees illustration adapted from The British Library collection:

Die Insel Rhodus, 1862.**

- Birds illustration adapted from: *The Fables of Aesop*, illustrated by Richard Heighway, c. 1894.+*
- Chained bird illustration adapted from The British Library collection: *Bishop, the bird man's book, on the care and management of birds*, 1886.**
- Birds on a branch illustration adapted from The British Library collection: *Woodland Romances; or, Fables and Fancies*, 1877.**
- Tightrope illustration adapted from The British Library collection: *When Life is Young: a collection of verse for boys and girls*, 1894.**
- Puppet illustration adapted from Flickr/Fondo Antiguo de la Biblioteca de la Universidad de Sevilla: Universal: *Lello universal em 2 volumes : novo diccionário encyclopédico luso-brasileiro / organizado e publicado pela Livraria Lello sob a direcçao de Joao Grave e Coelho Netto. - Porto : Lello & Irmao*, 'Fantoches', 1940. Creative Commons (https://creativecommons.org/licenses/by/2.0/)
- Mausoleum illustration adapted from Wikimedia Commons: *Unsterblichkeit*, Hermann von Kaulbach, 1888.^^ *
- Mice and cat illustrations adapted from: *The Fables of Aesop*, illustrated by Richard Heighway, c. 1894.+*
- Bug illustration adapted from Flickr/Internet Book Image photostream: *An encyclopædia of agriculture [electronic resource]*, 1831.**
- Eye illustration adapted from The British Library collection: *Footprints of the Lion, and other stories of travel ... With ... illustrations from photographs, etc*, 1897.**
- Rat illustration adapted from The British Library collection: *Travels in Africa during the years 1875-1878*, 1890.**
- Dish illustration adapted from *3,800 Early Advertising Cuts: Deberny Type Foundry*, 1991. Dover Publications, Inc.
- Soldiers illustration adapted from Wikimedia Commons: *Abreast*, Archives of Pearson Scott Foresman, donated to the Wikimedia Foundation, date unknown. This work has been released into the public domain by its author, Pearson Scott Foresman. This applies worldwide.
- Copernicus illustration adapted from Wikimedia Commons: *Nicolaus Copernicus*, Norsk bokmål. Unknown date.^^*
- Aristarchus illustration adapted from Wikimedia Commons: *10th century CE Greek copy of Aristarchus of Samos's 2nd century BCE calculations of the relative sizes of the Sun, Moon and the Earth.* ^^*
- Galileo MS image adapted from Wikimedia Commons: *Image of a*

draft letter written by Galileo Galilei to Leonardo Donato, Doge of Venice, August, 1609.^*

- Corset image adapted from Wikimedia Commons: Anti-masturbation corset. Illustration of a French book written by Guillaume Jalade-Lafond, title translated: *Thoughts about manufacturing self-made corsets and girdles to come up against the harmful habit of masturbation,* c. 1815.+*

- Buddha images adapted from Wikimedia Commons: *Kushan coins of the "Shakyamuni Buddha".* Personal drawing. World Imaging. Uploaded August, 2006. Permission is granted to copy, distribute and/or modify this document under the terms of the GNU Free Documentation License, Version 1.2 or any later version published by the Free Software Foundation. Creative Commons (https://creativecommons.org/licenses/by-sa/2.0/deed.en)

- Church illustration adapted from The British Library collection: *Geographisch-historisches Handbuch von Bayern,* 1895. No known copyright restrictions.

- Pastoral illustration adapted from Wikimedia Commons: *The Pastorals of Virgil, copy 1, object 6 Illustrations of Imitation of Eclogue,* woodcut by William Blake, c. 1821.^*

- Bishop illustration adapted from Wikimedia Commons: *Study of a Seated Bishop,* Belisario Corenzio, c. 1625.^*

- Snake illustration adapted from *Animals: 1,419 Copyright-Free Illustrations of Mammals, Birds, Fish, Insects, etc. A Pictorial Archive from Nineteenth-Century Sources.* 1979, Dover Publications, Inc.

- Characters adapted from The British Library collection: *The Political drama. [A series of caricatures.] - caption: "The five plagues of the country',* Charles Jameson Grant, c. 1834.**

- Crown illustration adapted from *3,800 Early Advertising Cuts: Deberny Type Foundry,* 1991. Dover Publications, Inc.

- Carl illustration adapted from The British Library Collection: *Absolutely True,* written and illustrated by Irving Montagu, 1893.**

- Farmer illustration adapted from: *The Fables of Aesop,* illustrated by Richard Heighway, c. 1894.+*

- Dog illustration adapted from *Animals: 1,419 Copyright-Free Illustrations of Mammals, Birds, Fish, Insects, etc. A Pictorial Archive from Nineteenth-Century Sources.* 1979, Dover Publications, Inc.

- Thinker illustration adapted from The British Library: *Lyrics of ancient Palestine. Poetical and pictorial illustrations of the Old Testam ... history,* illustrations drawn by A. de Neuville, P. Skelton, J. Wolf ... and others, 1873.**

- Knife illustration adapted from The British Library: *Comment j'ai retrouvé Livingstone ... Ouvrage traduit de l'anglais ... par Mme H. Loreau, etc,* 1874.**
- Circumcision illustration adapted from Wikipedia: *The Circumcision of Christ,* detail from *Twelve Apostles Altar (Zwölf-Boten-Altar),* Friedrich Herlin, c. 1465.^*
- Title graphic adapted from The British Library: *New Operas, with comical Stories, and Poems, on several occasions, never before printed, being the remaining pieces, written by Mr D,* 1721.**
- Woman on cliff illustration adapted from Wikimedia Commons: *Marvels of the new West,* 1887.**
- Cowboy illustration adapted from Wikimedia Commons: *Barton Bros Circus and Wild West,* programme cover, 1914.**
- Judge graphic adapted from The British Library: *Los Españoles pintados por sí mismos. Por varios autores. Adornada con cien grabados,* 1851.**
- Cricket illustration adapted from The British Library: *The British Miscellany: or, coloured figures of new, rare, or little known animal subjects, etc. vol. I., vol. II,* 1806.**
- Couple illustration adapted from The British Library: *A collection of pamphlets, handbills, and miscellaneous printed matter* - caption: 'Strand Theatre', signed NIOBE, 1892.**
- Aristocrat illustration adapted from The British Library collection: *Songs ... in an entirely new ... burletta ... called Tom and Jerry, or Life in London ... founded on P. E.'s work, etc,* 1820.**
- Terror illustration adapted from Wikimedia Commons: from *Charles Darwin's The Expression of the Emotions in Man and Animals.* Caption reads "FIG. 20.—Terror, from a photograph by Dr. Duchenne, 1872.+*
- Mirror illustration adapted from *3,800 Early Advertising Cuts: Deberny Type Foundry,* 1991. Dover Publications, Inc.
- Flim/Flam illustrations adapted from *3,800 Early Advertising Cuts: Deberny Type Foundry,* 1991. Dover Publications, Inc.
- Bugler illustration adapted from *3,800 Early Advertising Cuts: Deberny Type Foundry,* 1991. Dover Publications, Inc.
- Bronco illustration adapted from *Animals: 1,419 Copyright-Free Illustrations of Mammals, Birds, Fish, Insects, etc. A Pictorial Archive from Nineteenth-Century Sources.* 1979, Dover Publications, Inc.
- Jack in the box illustration adapted from The British Library collection: *When Life is Young: a collection of verse for boys and girls,* 1894.**
- Alchemy illustration adapted from The British Library collection:

A treatise on the distillation of Coal-Tar and Ammoniacal Liquor, and the separation from them of valuable products. [Translated from the German.], 1882. **

• Scientist illustration adapted from The British Library collection: *The Half Hour Library of Travel, Nature and Science for young readers,* 1896.**

• Monkey illustration adapted from *Animals: 1,419 Copyright-Free Illustrations of Mammals, Birds, Fish, Insects, etc. A Pictorial Archive from Nineteenth-Century Sources.* 1979, Dover Publications, Inc.

• Composite man falling off the world illustration adapted from The British Library collection: *The Colombian Navigator or Sailing Directory for the American Coasts and the West-Indies,* 1839.** and The British Library collection: *Local Poetry. Songs and poems, relating to the town and county of Newcastle upon Tyne, or incidents connected therewith,* 1780.**

• Box illustration adapted from The British Library collection: *Voyage d'exploration sur le littoral de la France et de l'Italie,* 1861.**

• Lounging illustration adapted from Wikimedia Commons: *Laziness,* Félix Emile-Jean Vallotton, 1895. The author died in 1925, so this work is in the public domain in its country of origin and other countries and areas where the copyright term is the author's life plus 80 years or less.*

• Shoes illustration adapted from *3,800 Early Advertising Cuts: Deberny Type Foundry,* 1991. Dover Publications, Inc.

• Rat illustration adapted from *Animals: 1,419 Copyright-Free Illustrations of Mammals, Birds, Fish, Insects, etc. A Pictorial Archive from Nineteenth-Century Sources.* 1979, Dover Publications, Inc.

• Death illustration adapted from The British Library Collection: *Death's Doings; consisting of numerous original compositions, in prose and verse, the ... contributions of various writers; principally intended as illustrations of twenty-four plates designed and etched by R. Dagley,* 1827.**

• Cursive script by Elaine Stanley, 2016.

• Drop cap L illustration adapted from: *The Fables of Aesop,* illustrated by Richard Heighway, c. 1894.+*

• Stalactite illustration adapted from Wikimedia Commons: *Line art representation of Stalactites,* date unknown. This work has been released into the public domain by its author, Pearson Scott Foresman. This applies worldwide.

• Elk illustration adapted from Wikimedia Commons: *Ciervo pintado en la cueva de Las Chimenesas, del monte Castillo, Puente Viesgo,* self work (hand-made sketch), José-Manuel Benito Álvarez —> Locutus Borg, 1985. This work has been released into the public domain by its author, Locutus Borg. This applies worldwide.

- Learner illustration adapted from The British Library collection: *When Life is Young: a collection of verse for boys and girls*, 1894.**
- Icarus illustration adapted from Wikimedia Commons: *Icarus, Hendrick Goltius after Cornelis van Haarlem*, 1588.^*
- Ship illustration adapted from The British Library collection: *When Life is Young: a collection of verse for boys and girls*, 1894.**
- Hammer illustration adapted from The British Library collection: *The Bab Ballads, with which are included Songs of a Savoyard ... With 350 illustrations by the author*, W. S. (William Schwenck) Gilbert, 1898.**
- Woman and man illustrations adapted from The British Library collection: *Love Lyrics and Valentine Verses, for young and old*, 1875.**
- Wilbur Wright letter illustration adapted from: *Octave Chanute Papers: Special Correspondence--Wright Brothers*, 1900, Wilbur and Orville Wright Papers, Manuscript Division, Library of Congress, Washington, D.C.
- Wright Brothers illustration adapted from Wikimedia Commons: *Wright glider, Wilbur at left side, Orville at right; Kitty Hawk, North Carolina*, 1901. This media file is in the public domain in the United States.*
- Woman illustration adapted from Wikimedia Commons: *Head of a woman expressing desire (left); head of a woman expressing hope (right).* Etching by B. Picart, 1713, after C. Le Brun. Creative Commons (https://creativecommons.org/licenses/by/4.0/deed.en)
- Mehitabel illustration adapted from author's collection: *Mehitabel*, 1988.
- Butterfly illustration adapted from The British Library: *Peeps into the Haunts and Homes of the Rural Population of Cornwall. Being reminiscences of Cornish character and characteristics, etc.*, 1879.**
- Surfer illustration adapted from Wikimedia Commons: *Hawaii, The Surf Rider*, Charles W. Bartlett, 1921. The author died in 1940, so this work is in the public domain in its country of origin and other countries and areas where the copyright term is the author's life plus 75 years or less.*
- Shell illustration adapted from *Animals: 1,419 Copyright-Free Illustrations of Mammals, Birds, Fish, Insects, etc. A Pictorial Archive from Nineteenth-Century Sources.* 1979, Dover Publications, Inc.
- Plum tree illustration adapted from *Plants: 2,400 Royalty-Free Illustrations of Flowers, Trees, Fruits and Vegetables*, 1988. Dover

Publications, Inc.

- Seed illustration adapted from Wikimedia Commons: *Dandelion seed head closeup*, 2009. This image, which was originally posted to Flickr. com, was uploaded to Commons using Flickr upload bot on 14:48, 30 April 2010 (UTC) by Mindmatrix. Creative Commons https:// creativecommons.org/licenses/by/2.0/deed.en)
- Planet illustration adapted from *3,800 Early Advertising Cuts: Deberny Type Foundry*, 1991. Dover Publications, Inc.
- Darwin notebook illustration adapted from Wikimedia Commons: *Charles Darwin's 1837 sketch, his first diagram of an evolutionary tree from his First Notebook on Transmutation of Species (1837) on view at the Museum of Natural History in Manhattan.*+ *
- Thinker illustration adapted from Wikimedia Commons: *Moça com Livro*, Almeida Júnior , between 1850 and 1899.^*
- Bridge illustration adapted from Wikimedia Commons: *Illustration from "The Scenery and Antiquities of Ireland"*, engraving by William Henry Bartlett, c. 1842.+*.
- Bicyclist illustration adapted from The British Library collection: *The Wheels of Chance. A holiday adventure, etc*, 1896.**
- Dancer illustration adapted from The British Library collection: *L'Espagne ... Illustrée de 309 gravures dessinées sur bois par Gustave Doré*, 1874.**
- Doc Lavan illustration adapted from Wikimedia Commons: *Exhibits W461 baseball card for Doc Lavan*, 1921. This media file is in the public domain in the United States.*
- Blue jay illustration adapted from *Animals: 1,419 Copyright-Free Illustrations of Mammals, Birds, Fish, Insects, etc. A Pictorial Archive from Nineteenth-Century Sources*. 1979, Dover Publications, Inc.
- Poppy illustration adapted from The British Library collection: *Selections from the literary and artistic remains of Paulina Jermyn Trevelyan, first wife of Sir W. C. Trevelyan*, 1879.**
- Cow illustration adapted from Flickr/ Internet Archive Book Images: *An encyclopaedia of agriculture*, c. 1831.**
- Banner illustration adapted from The British Library collection: *The Mirror of Music. [A story.]*, 1895.**
- Lighthouse illustration adapted from Wikimedia Commons: *Le Phare d'Alexandrie, selon gravure du XIXè siècle*, gravure sur bois de Sidney Barclay, 1880.+*
- Bird illustration adapted from Wikimedia Commons: *A Cape Petrel taking off from the sea in the Southern Ocean, near Clarence Island, South Shetland Islands, Antarctica*, 2011. This image was originally

Please visit

www.thebeatinpath.com

to download questions and topics for discussion, and to find extras and other details about The Beatin' Path!

CPSIA information can be obtained
at www.ICGtesting.com
Printed in the USA
FSOW01n1324130117
29613FS